How to Use Self-Muscle Testing As an Accurate Multidimensional Divination Tool

By George C. Georgiou

Self-Published by George C. Georgiou
http://EvolveWithGCG.com/

COPYRIGHT PAGE

Title: How to Use Self-Muscle Testing as an Accurate Multidimensional Divination Tool
Author & Publisher: George C. Georgiou
Published in **2025**

http://EvolveWithGCG.com/

A catalog record of this book is available at the Cyprus State Library.
ISBN (Print Edition): **978-9925-8238-3-3**
First Print Edition

Disclaimer:
The content of this book is intended for informational, experiential, and entertainment purposes only. The advice and strategies presented in this book may not be applicable to every situation. This work is provided with the understanding that neither the author nor the publisher shall be held liable for any outcomes resulting from the use of the information contained herein. Readers are encouraged to exercise their own judgment and seek professional guidance where appropriate.

DEDICATION

To my wonderful parents, Harry and Joana, for your unwavering support and understanding. I am eternally grateful and will always hold you in my heart with love.

To those striving to reach their full potential,
and to those who are, or aspire to be, powerful forces of goodness and service.

ACKNOWLEDGMENTS

To my dear friend Kelma D. Batong, who skillfully stepped into the role of photographer, capturing every self-muscle testing position with care and precision, and kindly modeled for the demonstrations.

To our family dog Max, who agreed to participate in a photo shoot with minimal bribery. Your patience and photogenic paws did not go unnoticed. 😊

*And to my AI sidekick ChatGPT **3.5**, thank you for tirelessly proofreading without a single coffee break or complaint, creating my book cover images, and even authoring **3** pages within Chapter **19**. You are the man* 😊

Join My Inner Circle

Ready to unlock your full potential and accelerate your spiritual evolution? My biweekly newsletters serve as your gateway to powerful insights, drawing from both ancient wisdom and modern discoveries in science and spirituality.

Each issue delivers carefully curated gems; the most impactful tools, teachings, and perspectives I've explored — all distilled for clarity and practicality. No fluff, no overwhelm, just the essence of what truly works for personal transformation.

I do the deep digging so you don't have to, because I value your time as much as your growth.

Join now at *http://EvolveWithGCG.com/newsletter/*

Let's evolve together!

Table of Contents

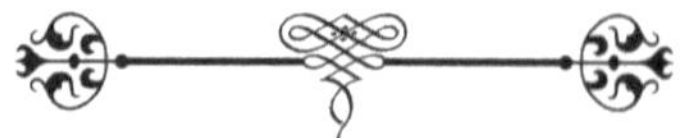

"It is the nature of our chosen reality and evolving consciousness that we cannot help but seek answers until we remember our infinite source."

— George C. Georgiou

HOW TO READ THIS BOOK

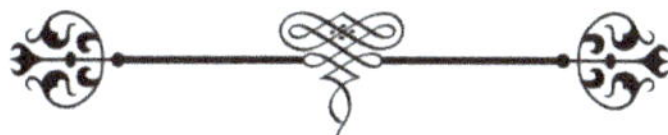

As you embark on this journey through the pages of this book, I encourage you to read it sequentially, from cover to cover, without skipping ahead. The structure and order of the chapters have been meticulously planned with you, the newcomer to this subject, in mind. Each concept builds upon the previous, laying a foundation for a deeper understanding as you progress.

Therefore, resist the urge to jump directly to individual chapters as if they were isolated topics. They are interconnected and designed to be understood as part of a whole. Of course, once you've completed the initial reading, feel free to revisit sections as standalone references.

I also consider the "About the Author" section to be of significant importance. Understanding the author's background, experiences, and the journey that led to the knowledge shared in this book can enhance your trust and connection with the material, especially if you find yourself skeptical about the content or its origins.

Self-muscle testing is not just a concept but a skill that requires practice. Like any skill, proficiency comes with practice, not just from reading.

To my fellow seekers of your full potential, I wish you a fulfilling and enlightening experience. May this book meet and exceed your expectations!

ABOUT THE AUTHOR

- George C. Georgiou -

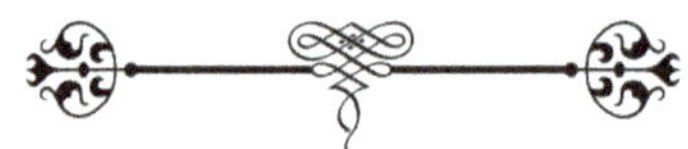

I believe that when it comes to spiritual matters, a certain level of trust must exist between the author and the reader. One way to build trust is by getting to know a person a little better, including their background, training, and life experiences.

So this is what I will attempt to do here, and even though my life was very episodic and full from the start, I will only include the absolute highlights.

I was born and raised in the Republic of Cyprus in 1974. As a child, I remember staying at home glued to the TV. I used to love it; I could sit in front of that screen all day long without a problem. Even the most pivotal event in my life, something that profoundly affected me and has shaped my path ever since, occurred while I was watching TV.

I believe I was around eight or nine years old when I saw the first episode of a TV series called *Battlestar Galactica*. When I watched that first episode, something within me was awakened. I felt instantly connected to life in space, to the existence aboard those massive motherships, and I experienced a strange sense of nostalgia.

That is the closest way I can describe it. That moment truly shaped my life, because from then on, almost all of my habits and actions have revolved around wanting to reconnect with that experience. It became my driving passion above all else.

From the age of twelve, I began reading every book I could find about aliens and UFOs. As I grew older, that passion expanded into other subjects, including paranormal phenomena, esoteric teachings, ancient mysteries, suppressed discoveries, and free energy, among others.

At age twenty, I stumbled upon a transformative book in a secondhand bookstore: *Hypnotism, Its Facts, Theories, and Related Phenomena* by Carl Sextus, first published in 1893. This work unveiled the extraordinary capabilities of the human mind and launched me onto a path of deep exploration and discovery. The content was astonishing, filled with mystical and supernatural demonstrations of hypnotism. It was my first encounter with such rare and intriguing concepts and abilities of the mind that I had never imagined were possible. I saw this book as revolutionary, far ahead of its time, and even challenging the views of the modern world.

Inspired by this groundbreaking work, I committed myself to exploring the vast potential of the human mind, setting out on what would become a lifelong journey of investigation and enlightenment.

At twenty-two, I relocated to Melbourne, Australia, to pursue Chiropractic studies at RMIT University. Three years later, I began attending the Sunday morning services at The Church of Spiritual Unity, part of the Spiritualist Church. Additionally, every other Thursday night, I participated in their Psychic Development Circle.

If you are wondering when I was first introduced to spirituality and began honing my psychic abilities, this was the pivotal moment.

During my final four years in Australia, I was fortunate to discover Pranic Healing. I completed all available courses, and remarkably, for about half of them, I was taught by the founder, Grand Master Choa Kok Sui. These experiences were unforgettable and transformative.

In these courses, I explored the intricate anatomy of the spiritual body, learning about various afflictions and their remedies. I also developed proficiency in key practices, including psychic protection, self-healing, distant healing, and the therapeutic use of crystals.

Concluding what I call my Australian chapter, in my final year there, 2002, I enrolled in a clinical hypnosis certification course at the Academy of Hypnotic Science in Melbourne. This was a milestone I had eagerly anticipated ever since reading Carl Sextus' book.

Upon returning to Cyprus in 2003, I secured various loans to establish my chiropractic practice, purchase a car, and acquire the necessary equipment. Initially, business was slow, as chiropractic services were relatively unknown in the area at the time. It took more than two years to develop a steady flow of patients that could cover my loan payments. Fortunately, my certification as a clinical hypnotherapist, along with the local demand for smoking cessation and my specialization in hypno-birthing, became unexpected lifelines during this period.

In 2010, the financial crisis hit Cyprus, profoundly impacting my business. Within seven months, my lifestyle had undergone a dramatic shift. I could no longer afford my secretary or the house I was renting, which led to my wife and me being squeezed into the apartment I used for work, with our bed awkwardly placed in the kitchen.

During these troublesome times, I faced severe insomnia, depression, and anxiety. Nights became endless battles for sleep, tossing around until 4:30 AM when I would collapse from exhaustion, only to be awakened again at 7:30 AM.

Desperate for some real rest, I turned to prescribed medication, taking significant doses just to eke out four to five hours of sleep.

Amidst these struggles, my personal life took a final hit: the divorce from my wife, adding a painful endnote to an already devastating chapter.

A few months later, I stumbled upon some meditation books I had bought years ago but never opened. This sparked a realization. If sleep eluded me, perhaps meditation could serve as a substitute.

Initially, learning to meditate was challenging, especially with a restless mind. However, I was fortunate to have excellent guidance through the books authored by Swamis and Yogis, for which I remain deeply grateful.

After a month of diligent self-training, despite the difficulties, I reached a point where I could lie in bed for four hours each night, completely still in a meditative state, meaning without tossing around or being besieged by endless thoughts. By around 3 AM, I would drift into sleep for about 2.5 hours.

This new routine worked wonders for me, leaving me feeling rejuvenated each morning, alert and clear-minded, with a surge of energy. Remarkably, this practice yielded consistent results nightly. Following my doctor's advice, I was eventually able to wean off the sleep medication.

Learning and practicing meditation marked a significant milestone in my life, offering solace during challenging times. My practice evolved from merely calming my mind and body to becoming a gateway for accessing my psychic abilities. This included regularly engaging with my Higher Self and my 6th-dimensional self. I provide details about these two connections in Chapters 10.3. 6th-Dimensional Self and 10.4. Higher Self.

These profound collaborations allowed me to overcome numerous limiting factors and barriers from past lifetimes. I gained the ability to receive instant answers to complex questions, innovate, write books, design a superior course, alter undesirable soul contracts, and secure protection against various threats, among other advantages.

Another pivotal aspect of my life has been my commitment to practicing CE-5, also known as HICE (Human-Initiated Contact Experiences), where you essentially meditate and telepathically send an invitation to extraterrestrial races found throughout the Universe to come and interact with you. Over the years, this practice has led to numerous ET encounters.

While most experiences have been positive, some have been negative, and others have been extraordinary, such as discovering that I had ET hybrid children and the visitation of two ET crafts, one approaching as close as 200 meters horizontally to us, and another, a huge one, silently gliding above us. Both events took place in a remote area on a mountain, which has been my regular place for contacting CE-5.

If I write another book in the future, I have a clear idea what it will be all about!

Throughout my life, I have encountered numerous milestones and challenges, each shaping my journey in a unique way. While this book is not an autobiography, I hope sharing these experiences provides valuable insights into my background and the knowledge I present.

Namaste,

George C. Georgiou

"The mystery of life isn't a problem to solve, but a reality to experience."

— Frank Herbert, Dune

PREFACE

Years ago, I hesitated to write and publish this book because I worried it might reduce attendance at my workshops. But now, as I embark on major life changes — retiring from my primary profession, concluding my workshops, and relocating abroad — I realize I have no excuse left not to write it. More importantly, I came to realize the importance of documenting and sharing the profound wisdom I have gathered over the years from various Higher Sources of Knowledge and Wisdom. Withholding this information would not only feel selfish but also unethical, given its potential to help so many people.

This book is designed to teach you how to connect with various dimensions where Higher Sources of Knowledge and Wisdom reside. Using self-muscle testing as your divination tool, you will learn how to receive answers directly, without needing to consult mediums or channelers, or to enroll in countless classes and workshops aimed at developing psychic abilities.

My workshops, titled "Accessing the Akashic Records with the GCG Divination System," lasted a day and a half. They focused primarily on two Higher Sources: the subconscious mind and the Akashic Records.

Over time, however, I encountered many more Higher Sources. I became familiar with them not only through direct access, but also through insights received from my Higher Self and the Akashic Records. In this book, I introduce you to eight of these Higher Sources and explain that they are only a glimpse of what is possible. There are infinitely more, and you can connect with them using the same method taught for the others.

CHAPTER 1

Introduction: Embrace Your Infinite Potential

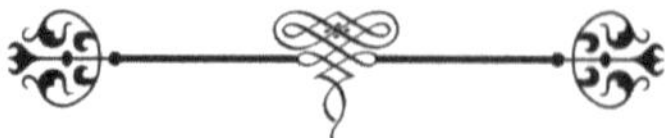

Welcome to a defining moment in your personal and spiritual development. This is more than the start of a book; it marks the commencement of a transformative adventure designed to broaden your horizons and enhance your innate abilities. Here, we will delve into the capabilities that lie within your full potential that may have awaited recognition and activation throughout your life.

It is time to embrace a profound truth. You inherently possess the ability to access realms and sources of knowledge beyond the limits of our physical reality. This capability is neither mere fiction nor arcane mysticism. It is a fundamental aspect of our advanced human evolution. Your DNA, a sophisticated and intricate blueprint, holds multidimensional attributes that enable you to explore and connect with diverse dimensions, unlocking access to vast reservoirs of knowledge. We can only hope that this newfound knowledge will be used exclusively to enhance our well-being and that of our planet.

Our advanced human evolutionary status is not just a theoretical notion. This is evidenced by the array of Extra Sensory Perceptions (ESPs) and psychic abilities we all possess, often lying dormant, waiting to be awakened. Abilities such as telepathy, clairvoyance, clairaudience, psychometry, remote viewing, astral projection, channeling, bilocation, and even teleportation are clear markers that we have reached an advanced stage in our evolution.

The idea of accessing Higher Sources of Knowledge and Wisdom, such as the Akashic Records, our Higher Self, or Oversoul, may seem reserved for only the chosen few—those mystics and sages who have dedicated their lives to spiritual ascension.

This is a great misconception. With your highly evolved DNA, you are inherently equipped to connect with these multidimensional realms in many ways.

This book provides everything you need: theory, principles, clear instructions, and photos that demonstrate how to utilize your muscular system and mind to interact with and retrieve information from Higher Sources of Knowledge and Wisdom.

I will show you how to use your mind and a technique called self-muscle testing as tools and conduits to access Higher Sources of Knowledge and Wisdom, regardless of their plane of existence.

As you embark on this journey through these pages, remember that this book is more than just an instructional manual; it is an invitation to transcend your perceived limitations and rediscover your true, multidimensional self!

"The mind is like a parachute - it works only when it is open."

— Frank Zappa

CHAPTER 2

What is Muscle Testing?

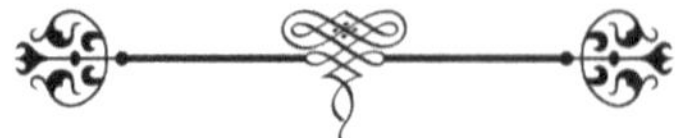

Muscle testing, within a clinical or medical examination context, is a method used to evaluate the strength of muscles and their associated tendons. This assessment is crucial for diagnosing and understanding the capacity of muscles to generate force. The evaluation uses a grading system with labels ranging from "zero" (no muscular activity) to "normal," "trace," "poor," "fair," and "good," or a numerical scale from 0 to 5. As revealed through this testing, muscle function impairments can stem from pathological disorders affecting various bodily systems, including the musculoskeletal, nervous, cardiovascular, and pulmonary systems.

Originating from the work of orthopaedic surgeon Robert W. Lovett in the early 1900s, muscle testing has become a fundamental part of physical examinations. For instance, in my former chiropractic practice, I often employed muscle testing to identify the underlying cause of specific symptoms. Consider a patient experiencing severe lower back pain with shooting pain down the legs. By assessing the muscle strength in the legs, which are innervated by lumbar nerves, I could determine whether the symptoms might be due to nerve impingement and, if so, at which specific lumbar level the issue is occurring. Conversely, if the muscles exhibit normal strength and reflexes, it suggests that the pain's root cause is not neurological, prompting further investigation into other possible causes.

It's important to note that the human body comprises approximately 320 pairs of muscles. This means each muscle has a corresponding counterpart on the opposite side of the body, allowing for a comprehensive and symmetrical assessment during muscle testing.

CHAPTER 3

Understanding the Five Types of Muscle Testing

Muscle testing is a versatile technique employed in various contexts, each with its own unique application and method. Here's an overview of the five types:

a) Hetero-muscle Testing: The picture below shows me performing a hetero-muscle test on a patient who reported shoulder pain after playing tennis. This is part of a typical physical examination conducted by a doctor to identify the specific area causing pain around the shoulder joint.

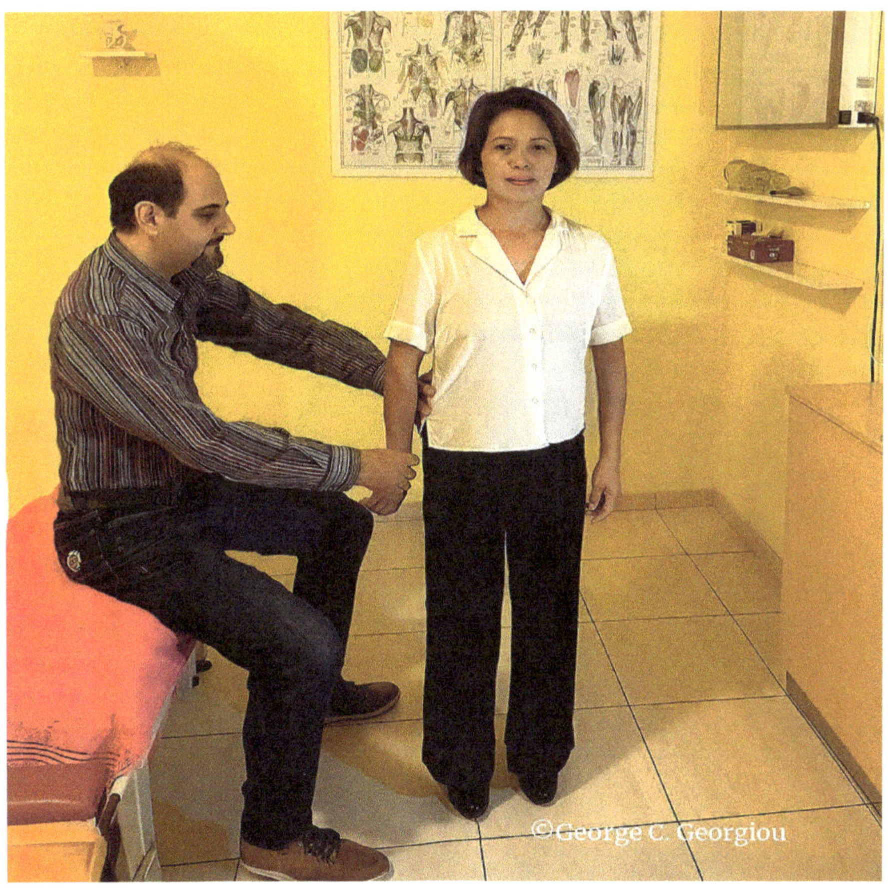

In this instance, I began by testing the Latissimus Dorsi muscle, which inserts at the back of the shoulder. With the patient's arm fully extended and rotated inward, I applied gentle resistance just above the wrist. The patient showed adequate strength and no pain, indicating the muscle and its tendon were not involved. I then proceeded to examine other shoulder structures to identify the source of the pain.

b) Auto or Self-muscle Testing:

This type allows individuals to perform muscle testing on themselves, enabling them to assess their own muscle strength and condition personally. However, we will use self-muscle testing as a precise tool for divination. In Chapter 6, I explain how this is possible. Additionally, a significant portion of the book is dedicated to teaching you how to master this method, explore the various Higher Sources of Knowledge and Wisdom available to you, and how you can access them to receive instant answers whenever you need them.

c) Dynamometry Muscle Testing:

This type involves using a mechanical device to conduct a muscle test, which measures the force output of the tested muscle, expressed in pounds or kilograms. A common example of such a device is a grip or hand dynamometer. It provides precise and objective data and is typically used in clinical settings.

d) Surrogate Muscle Testing:

This type of muscle testing involves using a substitute or surrogate, someone who is physically healthy and agrees to have their muscles tested on behalf of another person who is unable to undergo muscle testing themselves due to physical or mental limitations.

This technique is especially useful for obtaining information from infants, young children, comatose patients, and others living with severe health impairments. I also include animals in this group, as they, too, are unable to express what they are feeling or where it hurts. Many pet owners have shared their frustration and heartbreak with me, explaining how veterinarians often resort to a series of costly and general tests, simply because the actual cause remains hidden.

Many pet owners initially attend my workshops for this very reason. Of course, after completing the workshop, their perspective broadens, and muscle testing their pets becomes just one of the many ways they apply self-muscle testing in their daily lives.

Surrogate testing is covered in detail in Chapter 20: Advanced Applications of Self-Muscle Testing for Divination.

e) Metaphysical Muscle Testing:

This refers to all applications of muscle testing that extend beyond the conventional context of assessing muscle function for its biological status. Whether we use hetero-muscle testing, self-muscle testing, dynamometry, or surrogate muscle testing, it is classified as meta-physical muscle testing if applied in unconventional contexts.

Examples include using muscle testing to gather information about a person, an animal, or an object from photographs, maps, or other sources; locating water; finding lost persons or treasures; and, of course, obtaining data from a Higher Source of Knowledge and Wisdom, which is the primary focus of this book. Ultimately, the possibilities of metaphysical muscle testing are limited only by your imagination!

One might say, "Wait a minute, this sounds a lot like dowsing!"

And the answer is yes! Both self-muscle testing and dowsing can serve as divination tools. Continue reading as I clarify this further, helping you gain a deeper understanding of what you're learning.

CHAPTER 4

Explaining Key Spiritual Terms

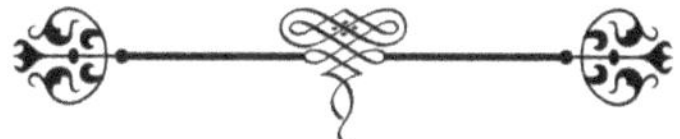

Divination: This term refers to the practice of obtaining knowledge and insight through supernatural or unconventional means, beyond our typical sensory perceptions.

Dowsing (or Rhabdomancy): Dowsing is an ancient form of divination performed with tools like rods or pendulums. Traditionally, it is used to locate subterranean resources such as water, oil, or minerals, but it can also be employed to obtain answers to questions.

Divination Tools: These are instruments or elements used to assist in divination practices.

Pendulum: A pendulum consists of a weighted object suspended from a chain or string. Often used in spiritual healing and divination, the pendulum acts as a responsive tool. When held stationary and questions are posed, it swings or rotates in specific directions corresponding to pre-determined responses.

Main Differences Between Dowsing and Self-Muscle Testing:

- Each technique utilizes its own distinct divination tools.

The divination tools for dowsing are pendulums, dowsing rods (e.g., L-Rods and Y-Rods), aurameters, and biotensors.

For self-muscle testing, the most commonly used parts of the body are the forearm, hands, and fingers.

- During dowsing, the dowser's mind focuses on what they wish to locate, such as water, gold, oil, or similar resources. In self-muscle testing, the practitioner connects to a part of us known as the subconscious mind.

In this book, I explain how we can choose and connect with a vast array of what I refer to as Higher Sources of Knowledge and Wisdom. In other words, the subconscious mind is just one database among many. Selecting the appropriate higher source based on your question or topic ensures more precise and accurate answers.

A Note on the Usage of Pendulums:

Many of my seminar participants who initially used pendulums for divination purposes later shared their experiences with me during follow-up discussions. Most of them admitted that, after learning self-muscle testing, it became their preferred method for obtaining answers to their questions. They chose to set aside their pendulums, using them only for specific healing systems they had previously learned.

There is one final term I want to clarify: 'Dimension.'

The word "dimension" can have many meanings depending on the context in which it is used, whether in everyday language, scientific fields such as mathematics and physics, or in spiritual discussions.

In the context of this book, and depending on how it is used, it can mean one of two things. First, it may refer to a reality or plane of existence, typically one that extends beyond our familiar four-dimensional framework of length, width, height, and time. The term "multi-dimensional" refers to the existence of many such realities or planes.

Second, it can describe the scale or scope of a particular level of consciousness. The highest of these is God-consciousness, which exists at the 13th dimension and encompasses all that is.

Here are some examples:

- Lucid dreams provide a glimpse into realms beyond our earthly experiences, often described as journeys into different "dimensions."
- We exist in a multi-dimensional universe.

- The Akashic Records reside within their own distinct dimension.
- The Over Soul is considered a 9th-dimensional entity, while Mother Earth is a 10th-dimensional entity.

And there you have it! Now you know the true meaning of the title of my book:

'How to Use Self-Muscle Testing as an Accurate Multidimensional Divination Method.'

"The mind, once stretched by a new idea, never returns to its original dimensions."

— Ralph Waldo Emerson

CHAPTER 5

Origins and Brief History of Applied Kinesiology (AK) and Kinesiology

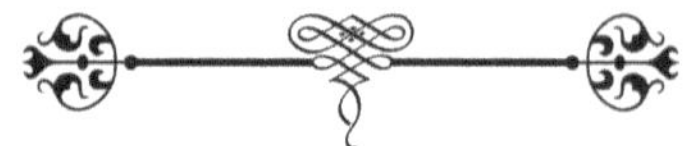

An American chiropractor, Dr. George Goodheart (1918-2008), revolutionized his field through extensive observation and innovative use of muscle testing. His work expanded the application of muscle testing beyond its conventional bounds to include the detection of structural, chemical, neurological, and psychological imbalances. Furthermore, he utilized muscle testing to tailor specific treatment plans for each patient.

These innovations form the cornerstone of what you would learn in an Applied Kinesiology (AK) or a Kinesiology course. I will detail the distinctions between these two fields shortly.

Dr. Goodheart's contributions were not limited to original techniques; he also integrated therapeutic modalities developed by other healthcare practitioners after proving their efficacy. This included osteopathic methods, such as Chapman's neurolymphatic points and various components from Traditional Chinese Medicine, including meridians and acupuncture points.

By compiling these diverse approaches, Dr. Goodheart established a cohesive framework for healthcare called Applied Kinesiology. In 1964, he formally introduced the Applied Kinesiology system and founded the 'Goodheart Study Group Leaders' to disseminate this knowledge among chiropractors.

This organization evolved over time and was rebranded as "The International College of Applied Kinesiology" (ICAK) in 1976. The ICAK now offers a variety of certification programs in Applied Kinesiology worldwide, primarily aimed at chiropractors and other healthcare professionals.

In 1979, John Thie, a student of Dr. Goodheart and a founding member of ICAK, sought to make the core techniques and principles of Applied Kinesiology accessible to the general public. He distilled AK concepts into a series of seminars titled 'Touch for Health.' Consequently, those not affiliated with ICAK are now commonly called "Kinesiology practitioners."

Over the past four decades, Dr. Goodheart's foundational system has inspired the development of numerous methodologies by practitioners of Applied Kinesiology and Kinesiology. These new approaches not only address a wide range of health issues but have also expanded into alternative fields such as energetics, spirituality, education, psychology, and many others.

"It has been my observation that most people get ahead during the time that others waste."

— Henry Ford

CHAPTER 6

History of Self-Muscle or Auto-Muscle Testing

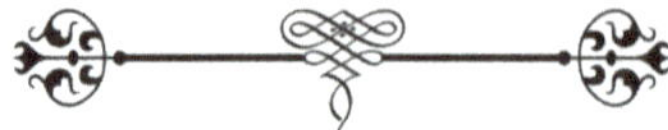

In my humble opinion, the origins of most hand/finger self-muscle testing techniques used today for divination or Metaphysical Muscle Testing can be traced back to 1977, when Professor Yoshiaki Omura, MD, discovered the "bi-digital O-ring test" (BDORT). Although he initially classified and demonstrated this technique as a form of hetero-muscle testing.

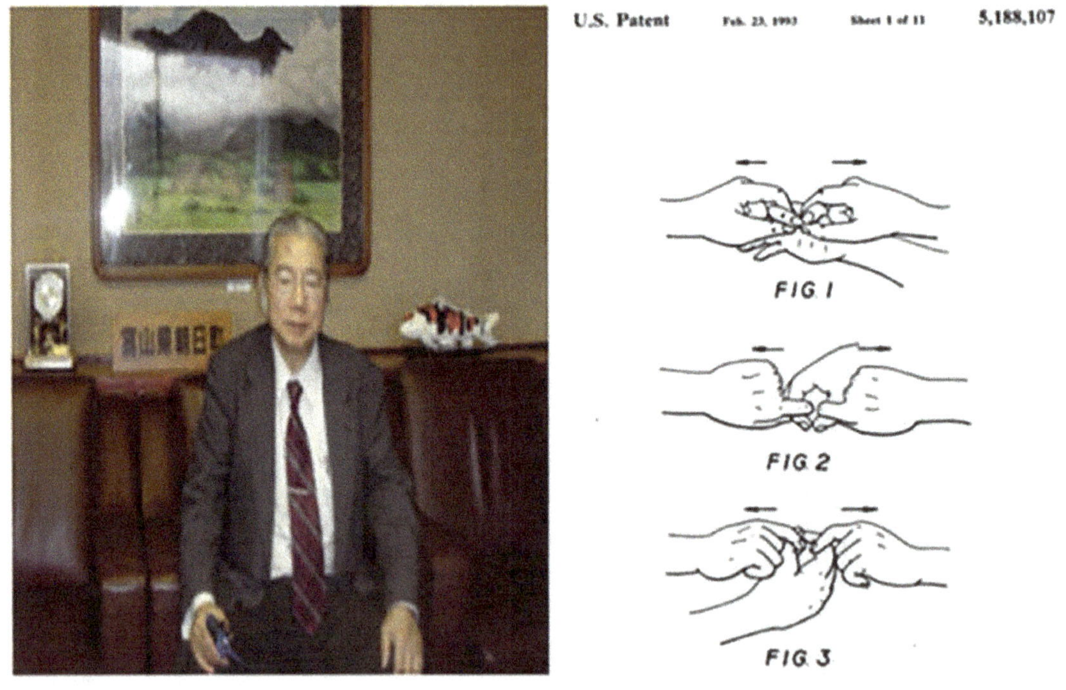

Image sources: https://bdort.org/research.html, https://patents.google.com/patent/US5188107

Professor Omura stated that applied kinesiology did not influence his technique, claiming that the two have fundamentally different bases and share little in common. According to him, BDORT is primarily an electromagnetic resonance test based on principles from physics, physical chemistry, and modern medical science.

However, despite these assertions, Professor Omura employed his technique for purposes similar to those of Applied Kinesiology, such as identifying bodily imbalances or diseases and determining appropriate treatments based on muscle test outcomes. Given the historical precedent and acknowledged awareness of Applied Kinesiology, I remain skeptical of his claim that he was not inspired by it.

To the best of my knowledge, Professor Omura was the first to apply self-muscle testing for metaphysical purposes, including analyzing patient photographs for diagnostic insights and detecting substances such as asbestos within house walls.

For further insight into Professor Omura's work, you can visit his academic and clinical showcase at http://bdort.org/research.html (Last accessed March 3, 2024). His contributions are significant, and I believe you will find them equally impressive upon reviewing his achievements and the video demonstrating his technique on an actual patient, available on his website.

"Go confidently in the direction of your dreams. Live the life you have imagined."

— Henry David Thoreau

CHAPTER 7

Three Core Principles of Muscle Testing

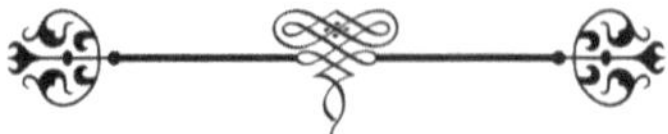

As a chiropractor and an Applied Kinesiologist with over 20 years of experience, I have distilled the essence of muscle testing within the contexts of both Applied Kinesiology and Kinesiology into three core principles. These principles apply across all types of muscle testing:

1. The Core Principle: During muscle testing, a true statement, a positive thought, or any element beneficial to the body will maintain the strength of a strong muscle or temporarily strengthen a previously tested weak muscle. Conversely, a false statement, a negative thought, or any harmful element will temporarily weaken a strong muscle or maintain the weakness in a previously tested weak muscle.

2. Universal Application: Muscle testing can be used to obtain a wide range of answers that extend beyond the physical state of our bodies and our own knowledge. This core principle, popularized by Dr. John Thie and Professor Omura, highlights the impressive capabilities of the human body, although the accuracy of these answers can vary.

But how is this possible? This question leads us to the third core principle, which is derived from the author's knowledge of spiritual matters and personal insights.

3. Connection with Spiritual Sources: This core principle suggests that humans have evolved to a stage where we can innately and naturally connect with various extra-dimensional Higher Sources of Knowledge and Wisdom. This advanced capacity explains our ability to obtain information that has not been previously known to us, in this case, through muscle testing.

A Note on the First Core Principle:

If you are new to muscle testing, don't worry about fully understanding this core principle just yet. Once we begin the hands-on, practical component of this technique, it will become clear!

> *"The best way to predict your future is to create it."*
>
> *— Peter Drucker*

CHAPTER 8

Eleven Reasons Why Self-Muscle Testing is the Superior Divination Method

Drawing on over 25 years of personal experience with self-muscle testing and various spiritual practices, I explain why I believe self-muscle testing is the leading divination method and a must-learn skill.

1. **Instant Answers:** Quickly access accurate insights on every aspect of life from various Higher Sources of Knowledge and Wisdom. The Akashic Records are just one of many!
2. **Surrogate Capability:** Facilitates testing on behalf of others.
3. **No Accessories Needed:** Free yourself from the burden of carrying pendulums, dowsing rods, or oracle cards.
4. **Rapid Mastery:** Unlike psychic abilities that may take years to develop, self-muscle testing can be mastered in just a weekend!
5. **Versatile:** Perform it anywhere without needing a quiet or specific environment.
6. **Unlimited Potential:** Your imagination is the only limit to its application.
7. **Transformative Impact:** Used wisely, it can fundamentally change your life!
8. **Spiritual Independence:** Become your own medium to access the answers you seek. Additionally, through consistent practice, you can gradually strengthen your extrasensory perceptions and abilities.

9. **Meditation-Friendly:** It can be performed with eyes closed, making it easy to integrate while in a meditative state.
10. **Complementary:** Easily integrates with other spiritual and energy practices.
11. **Cost-Effective:** It's ultimately free to use anytime.

"The man who acquires the ability to take full possession of his own mind, may take possession of anything else to which he is justly entitled."

— Andrew Carnegie

CHAPTER 9

Higher Sources of Knowledge and Wisdom: Understanding the Concept

What exactly are "Higher Sources of Knowledge and Wisdom"? This term, coined by the author, refers to distinct sources that store knowledge and wisdom in physical or non-physical forms, existing beyond our fourth-dimensional world. Among the most well-known of these sources are the Akashic Records.

Drawing from my experiences and insights, I assert that countless such sources exist, each representing or connected to a singular or collective consciousness.

A collective consciousness refers to a unified consciousness shared by a group or population, bound together by common origins, experiences, values, traditions, or stages of evolution.

For practical purposes, I have categorized these Higher Sources of Knowledge and Wisdom into two groups: those with a singular consciousness and those with a collective consciousness.

The most significant and widely recognized Higher Sources of Knowledge and Wisdom will be explained in this book. They will be presented with the assumption that your divination practice involves self-muscle testing.

Much of this information has been obtained directly through consultations with my Higher Self and the Akashic Records.

CHAPTER 10

Well-known Higher Sources of Knowledge and Wisdom with Singular Consciousness:

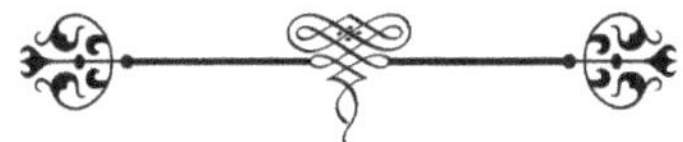

10.1. Subconscious Mind (also known as the Personal Unconscious Mind)
10.2. Inner Guides
10.3. 6th-Dimensional Self
10.4. Higher Self
10.5. Archangels and Angels
10.6. Akashic Records

10.1. Subconscious Mind (aka Personal Unconscious Mind)

Writing this section was challenging as the topic is vast enough to fill an entire book. While much valuable information is inevitably omitted, I've endeavored to provide the essentials and all the relevant details that can be useful when using self-muscle testing for divination purposes.

Despite our technological advancements, the precise physical location of the subconscious mind within the body remains elusive. However, its existence and functions are universally acknowledged.

It's crucial to distinguish between the brain and the mind: while they interact and are interconnected through a psychosomatic bridge, they represent different aspects of our being. Contrary to popular belief, memories are not stored in neurons in the brain. Even with the most powerful microscope on Earth, one cannot find memories within physical brain cells. Instead, memories reside within the vast and intangible dimension of the mind, which

Hinduism philosophy refers to as the mental body. Indeed, we possess several distinct yet interwoven bodies, much like Russian nesting dolls.

Although there are many "minds," I will keep this discussion simple by focusing on two: the conscious mind and the subconscious mind.

The conscious mind is active during wakefulness, collecting, receiving, and processing information from internal and external sources. It then analyzes this data to form conclusions, make decisions, and guide our actions.

Beneath the surface of conscious awareness lies the subconscious mind, far more potent and capable than its conscious counterpart.

It serves as a vast repository, recording every piece of information received through our senses, day and night. This includes, but is not limited to, memories, thoughts, dreams, feelings, experiences, and outcomes.

The subconscious mind remains in constant vigilance, staying awake, present, and active throughout our lifetime, unlike the conscious mind, which recedes during sleep or under anesthesia.

Our autonomic nervous system regulates involuntary physiological functions, including heartbeat, breathing, digestion, and body temperature, ensuring the body's internal environment remains stable. Thousands of bodily actions occur every second to maintain homeostasis, all of which the subconscious mind is constantly aware of and controls. This has been demonstrated through experiments conducted on subjects under hypnosis, during which the subconscious mind takes a dominant role.

Under these conditions, individuals can adjust their autonomic functions, such as increasing or decreasing their heart rate and body temperature, demonstrating the profound influence of the subconscious mind on the body's systems.

When you ask the subconscious mind a question, the answer is drawn from the information you have encountered, stored, and accumulated throughout your life, including knowledge from books, conversations, personal experiences, and other exposures. Additionally, the subconscious mind has a comprehensive understanding of your physical, emotional, mental, etheric, and energetic layers, making it a reliable Higher Source of Knowledge and Wisdom readily available for consultation.

By connecting to your subconscious mind through self-muscle testing, you can uncover insights and answers to questions such as:

- Am I deficient in certain vitamins or minerals?
- Do I have allergies to specific substances?
- Is consuming ...(particular food)... beneficial for me?
- Is this ...(physical, emotional, spiritual, or energetic)... activity beneficial or harmful to me?
- Is this ...(chakra, meridian, etheric layer, emotional layer)... healthy and balanced?
- For this issue, which of the following items will aid in restoring the health and balance of my ... (chakra, meridian, etheric layer, emotional layer)...?
- Do I have a particular disease or a predisposition to it?
- Which treatment option is better for ...(condition)...?

Another key fact about your subconscious mind is that it serves as our default Higher Source of Knowledge and Wisdom. If you perform self-muscle testing and choose not to connect to a particular source, meaning you choose to use the 'Casual Approach' to self-muscle testing for divination purposes, then the answers will automatically originate from your subconscious mind.

I have mentioned many impressive attributes of the subconscious mind and why it is considered one of the Higher Sources of Knowledge and Wisdom, even though it is the smallest database discussed in this book. However, I saved its most impressive and powerful attribute for last. I am confident that when I reveal it, you will be amazed and grateful to have such an incredible tool already embedded within you.

Under the right circumstances, your subconscious mind becomes even more powerful. This occurs when you transition from your normal, awake state, characterized by Beta brain waves, to Alpha or light-to-deep Theta brain waves, which are commonly experienced during meditation or hypnosis.

In these brain states, your subconscious mind not only selects the appropriate Higher Source of Knowledge and Wisdom based on your question but also establishes a connection with it. This process unfolds seamlessly and naturally, even though it involves linking you to dimensions beyond your own, where these higher sources reside. In this way, your subconscious acts as a bridge to realms beyond your usual dimension.

10.2. Inner guides

Before delving into the topic of Inner Guides, this is the perfect moment to briefly explore a related concept that will 'guide' us toward the main subject. It's essential to recognize that your spiritual journey, like everyone else's, is structured similarly to a school system. The key difference lies in focusing on actual experiences rather than theoretical knowledge, as hands-on experiences are the most effective way to learn and grow.

Much like a school system where teachers are assigned to specific age groups or levels, your inner guides, spirit guides, masters, and Angels are chosen and placed according to your stage of spiritual development and your unique needs.

Additionally, when a person advances or 'regresses' in their spiritual journey and moves beyond the range for which their current guide is suited, the Higher Self may replace the guide. Depending on the individual's circumstances and requirements, this change can be temporary or permanent. In our soul's journey, especially when we choose to incarnate in challenging environments like Earth, we often select experienced spirits to guide and assist us through life. These spirits, known as inner guides, reside within our energy field, typically near our chakras, and remain with us until we transition out of our physical existence.

Occasionally, our Higher Self perceives the need for additional spiritual assistance during significant life events, emotional turmoil, or pivotal decisions. In such cases, it reaches out to the astral world to bring in guides with specific expertise for a "special assignment." These temporary guides provide support until their purpose is fulfilled. One may have hundreds of these transient guides throughout a lifetime, even if unaware of their presence.

Each Inner Guide has lived thousands of lifetimes before attaining the wisdom and experience required for this role. They have gained deep knowledge of Earth's complexities, rules, terms, and conditions. With this understanding, they help humans navigate their journey and, in collaboration with the Higher Self, ensure steady progress along their soul path.

Inner Guides have had countless names throughout their existence. In their current evolutionary state, Inner Guides do not use names and are easily identified by their unique energy signature. However, in our reality, using a name is practical and necessary for clarity, as it eliminates any uncertainty about who you are interacting with. For this reason, if you choose to use your Inner Guides as a regular source of Higher Knowledge and Wisdom, I suggest giving them a name.

As mentioned, your Inner Guides have lived thousands of lifetimes, primarily as males or females. If they have lived in realms beyond Earth, they may have taken on additional forms, but male or female energy will typically remain more dominant in their essence. I mention this because you may prefer to connect with an Inner Guide whose energy aligns more closely with either male or female characteristics, depending on your needs.

The realm of spirit or inner guides is vast, encompassing a variety of types and ways of interaction. Numerous books and guided meditations are available to help those who wish to deepen their understanding and connection with these guides. In this book, I provide my approach to connecting with Inner Guides and obtaining instant answers through self-muscle testing.

I recommend starting by creating a basic profile for each of your Inner Guides and recording your answers to ensure you do not forget them. You can begin with the following questions:

- How many permanent Inner Guides do I have? (This is typically between three and seven.)
- Inner Guide number one, do you have predominantly male energy? (Use self-muscle testing to receive a "Yes" or "No.")
- Inner Guide number one, do you have predominantly female energy? (Use self-muscle testing to receive a "Yes" or "No.")
- Do you resonate with the name [insert name] I have chosen for you? (Use self-muscle testing to receive a "Yes" or "No.")

Repeat this process for the number of Inner Guides you have. Personally, I add the prefix "IG" to their names, which stands for "Inner Guide." For example, IG John, IG Samantha, and so on.

Connecting with your inner guides can uncover insights and answers to questions such as:

- How many special assignment guides are currently assisting me?
- What are your thoughts on my idea to...?
- Is now a good time to start my new project on...?
- Advice on personal relationships (partners, children, siblings, colleagues, etc.).
- Should I consider doing/going/changing... at this point in my life?

- How can I neutralize this emotion...?
- Where should I vacation to gain the most benefit?
- Where can I find a mentor about...?
- Which activities should I minimize or eliminate?
- Which activities should I prioritize or focus on?
- Is ... (list a specific factor)... contributing to my current condition?
- What is the root cause of my...?

Note:

When seeking assistance from your Inner Guides, an affirmative connection is generally expected unless the request involves harm to others. Generally speaking, there is always a chance of getting the wrong answers if you have not adequately prepared for your divination session. This includes instances where you have not fully neutralized personal biases or fears. In such cases, your ego, which may resist or hesitate about the experience, can take over and distort the answers from your chosen Higher Source of Knowledge and Wisdom. I explain how we can limit this possibility when discussing the Prompt Approach and the Extensive Approach in relation to connecting with your chosen Higher Source of Knowledge and Wisdom.

10.3. 6th-Dimensional Self

Your 6th-dimensional Self represents the most evolved and advanced version of your being. You are entirely free from physical constraints because you exist without a physical body and have no physical needs, ailments, or limitations. This version of you operates purely on energy and spirit, with nearly all psychic and spiritual abilities fully activated and functioning at an advanced level. The manifestation of desires becomes almost effortless.

In this heightened state, you have unrestricted direct access to most Higher Sources of Knowledge and Wisdom. You can seamlessly connect with other advanced entities, such as ascended masters, extraterrestrial beings, collective consciousnesses, and more.

In my spiritual journey, I communicate and collaborate daily with my 6th-dimensional self, who has accepted my invitation and become my Gatekeeper in various spiritual practices that require extra attention and protection.

I encourage you to connect with this profound aspect of yourself to gain insights comparable to those your inner guides offer. Experiment with both sources to see which aligns better with your energy and provides clearer guidance.

For those familiar with spiritual anatomy, such as auric layers, chakras, and meridians, delve deeper by asking specific questions:

- Are there any negative energies attached to me, such as spirit attachments or malignant implants?
- Which meridian is blocked, and at what level?

You can also seek guidance on awakening your psychic abilities. For example, compile a comprehensive list of specific meditations, mantras, mudras, and any other self-development techniques or courses you have encountered. Then you might ask, "6th-dimensional Self, which of these is the most effective way to develop my clairaudience? Which of these would be the most beneficial to me?" After asking each question, use muscle testing to evaluate each item on your list and determine which option would be best for you. This approach enables your 6th-dimensional Self to craft a personalized path for your spiritual and psychic growth.

10.4. Higher Self

The information shared below comes from my first three communications with my Higher Self during meditation on April 9, 10, and 11, 2011. I have chosen to include the extensive raw material as it was given to me, rather than offering a concise summary of its nature as I did with the other Higher Sources of Knowledge and Wisdom. There are many reasons for this, but two stand out above the rest.

First, there is a great deal of misinformation about what the Higher Self truly is and its role, much like the confusion surrounding the Akashic Records. The information you are about to read will dissolve any doubts or uncertainties you may have. You will finally gain a clear understanding of what the Higher Self is and the essential role it plays in your life.

Second, I believe the Higher Self is the greatest gift we receive when we incarnate on this planet. When I became aware of its communications, I experienced a profound acceleration in my spiritual growth within this spiritual school we call Earth.

I truly want you to have the same experience. I know without a doubt that the more people are able to clearly and freely communicate with their Higher Self, the safer and more harmonious our world will become.

****

Author: What exactly is a Higher Self?

Higher Self: In essence, we are the greater aspect of you that remains close to your home, known to you as the Source of Creation, when you choose to journey beyond it. Our role is vast and encompasses many responsibilities. Would you like to explore this further?

Author: Yes, please.

Higher Self: I would be happy to do so and will tailor my response to align with your spiritual path and level of understanding. I will also avoid mentioning the Great Divine Division, which led to duality, separation, and multiplicity, resulting in diverse expressions of the Divine, such as yourself and other beings having a soul, unless I am specifically asked to.

For all Creators who wish to experience other creations before exiting the Source of Creation, each individual soul leaves behind a larger part of themself.

Visualize yourself as one of the infinite Creators within the Source of Creation. As a Creator, your very nature is to create. At some point, you and many others choose to pause your creator roles and step away from the Source of Creation to explore and experience what has been created.

It is a long journey from your original home, spanning thousands of lifetimes. That is why you carefully designed a soul blueprint, complete with specific goals, rules, and conditions. Among these conditions, which I am sure you will find both fascinating and illuminating, is the fact that in third and fourth-dimensional lifetimes, most of your Creator abilities are temporarily deactivated. Much of your free will is also limited, allowing you to immerse yourself in the human experience fully. In higher dimensions, these abilities are gradually restored.

You also embedded several mechanisms within your blueprint to ensure you are guided and supported throughout your journey. One of the most vital of these is the Higher Self, the expanded part of you that remains beyond the physical realm. It oversees your blueprint, holding a complete view of all your lifetimes and guiding you toward experiences that align with your soul's greater purpose.

Given your love for the night sky and movies, here are two analogies that will help you understand the nature of the Higher Self even better.

Author: Thank you.

Higher Self: First, imagine a massive glowing star at the center of all existence. This is your home, the Source of Creation. From there, a bright beam of light travels a great distance and reaches another smaller luminous star, which we will call your Oversoul. From that point, yet another beam of light extends deeper into creation and reaches an even smaller luminous star, which is the Higher Self. From there, another beam extends further into creation and reaches an even smaller luminous star, which is the Lower Self, you. Everything surrounding the Higher and Lower Selves is simply creation.

Second, think of your Higher Self as the writer, producer, and in some ways, the director of each of your lifetimes.

Author: Does that mean you are responsible for all the bad things that have happened to me?

Higher Self: The short answer is yes. But remember, you and I are one, and we are one with all that is.

****

Author: Why do so many people feel disconnected from their Higher Selves or remain completely unaware of their existence? How is it that such a powerful and essential part of who we are is not naturally revealed to us?

Higher Self: This question, and like many others, best suited to be answered by the Higher Self, are being answered instantly all the time.

And before you protest what I just said, let me assure you that all your questions will be answered by the end of our conversation. This particular one is multifaceted, and I am ready to explore it with as much depth as you desire.

Remember, we are here to guide and support you on your journey so that you may learn and gather the experiences your soul seeks. But there would be little value if we were so close, so ever-present, that we dictated your every move. In that case, you would gain very little from the experience. On the other hand, if we remained distant and merely observed without ever offering guidance or support, that too would serve little purpose.

You must also understand that the kind of relationship you have with your Higher Self is a choice and a crucial part of your soul's education. To evolve, you will need to experience various types of relationships with us.

Communicating with you, the Lower Self, is of great importance to us, for if we cannot reach you, then we cannot fulfill our role. We make every effort to connect in ways that are always in harmony with the laws of your dimension. From your perspective, you could say that we communicate with you in two main ways: direct and indirect, but to us, it is all the same.

Direct communication may take the form of an inner voice, a sudden image or memory that carries meaning, a spontaneous thought, an insight, a moment of inspiration, or intuition. Not all such moments originate from the Higher Self, but many of them do. We also engage in what we call reality repainting. This is when we want to draw your attention to something, so we subtly alter your perceptions in ways designed to capture your awareness. A color might appear unusually vivid, a sound might shift in tone, a scent might suddenly arise without a source, or an object might momentarily vanish from your view. These are also direct messages from us.

Indirect communication mainly flows through synchronicities, those seemingly random yet deeply meaningful events we carefully orchestrate to bring specific messages or situations into your awareness. Most often, they are the result of ongoing collaboration between many Higher Selves and their associated Lower Selves.

At times, entire groups are guided to support or intersect with other groups in the service of a greater purpose. This intricate coordination happens continuously at the level of the Over Soul.

So, the real question we must ask is this: With all the ways we are reaching out to you, why is it that you still do not perceive us?

The answer is simple.

It depends on your environment and its level of pollution. I am talking about specific pollutants that interfere with the perception of our communication.

These pollutants cause messages from the Higher Self to go unheard, or if heard, to be ignored.

These pollutants tend to accumulate in environments dominated by fast-paced, artificial lifestyles. However, if you travel to regions of the planet where people live in harmony with nature and lead a more relaxed lifestyle, such as many native or tribal communities, you will find a different story.

Ask them about their communication with their Higher Self, and they will tell you how they were raised listening to that voice as clearly as if another person were right beside them, whispering in their ear. They will describe how that connection feels like a lifelong companion, a spiritual teacher, always offering guidance.

They may call it something else, such as the Great Spirit or the Great Hunter Within, but they refer to the same Higher Self.

So, as you can see, communication with the Higher Self varies greatly depending on your lifestyle and where you are on this planet.

Let us now explore a few of these pollutants that affect those living fast-paced and artificial lives, such as yourself and all of your friends, as far as we can tell.

We will also explore how these can be addressed, thus opening the way for clear and open communication between the Higher Self and the Lower Self.

Author: Why do you keep saying "we" instead of referring to yourself as "I"?

Higher Self: Because whenever I express something, especially on matters of a general spiritual nature, the answer comes from a shared source. It is the same truth offered by all Higher Selves. While the style and approach may vary for each of us as we tailor our expression to match the person's level of understanding, spiritual development, and even character, sometimes the essence remains the same. In one way or another, the Higher Self is always expressing itself to you.

Let us now return to the answer and begin with the first pollutant: misinformation!

There are two widely held false beliefs about the nature of the Higher Self. The first is that you are disconnected from it and must go through a process to reconnect. The second is that the Higher Self is somehow deactivated and needs to be activated through specific practices. Neither of these ideas is true and only serves to hinder your ability to communicate with us.

Please know this: your Higher Self is always with you and is always connected to you. The bond between us cannot be severed. It is constantly active and always working on your behalf.

That said, it is also true that during certain phases of your life or even entire lifetimes, this connection can feel weak, distant, or nearly non-existent. This, too, is part of your education.

Author: What kind of education would require the distancing of the Higher Self from the Lower Self?

Higher Self: The Higher Self is constantly involved in your personal growth and development. Sometimes, simply creating distance allows certain emotions to be experienced more easily, such as feelings of being lost, directionless, lonely, sad, depressed, panicked, or desperate. Though these moments are challenging, they are meaningful and rich with opportunities for growth.

When our high vibrational frequency is closer to you, it is only natural that you feel you are living your life with clarity, inspiration, and a strong sense of purpose. You feel guided, supported, and connected not only to yourself but also to something greater. Emotions such as inner peace, joy, trust, and confidence become easier to experience. Synchronicities occur more often, your intuition becomes sharper, and even in the face of challenges, you feel aligned and reassured that you are exactly where you are meant to be.

The Lower Self has much to learn by experiencing different degrees of closeness with the Higher Self.

Higher Self: Would you like to ask anything else about this matter?

Author: No, I am good for now.

Another set of pollutants that negatively interfere with someone's Higher Self Communication comes in the form of internal and external noise, an overwhelming flood of mental chatter, and the constant barrage of sounds from your modern world.

As I mentioned earlier, we utilize multiple channels to convey vital messages to you. But what happens when those channels are crowded with dozens or even hundreds of competing thoughts, emotions, and distractions?

Imagine this: one part of yourself keeps repeating an idea out of fear that it might be forgotten. Another is worrying about a problem. One part of you is busy calculating something. Another is stewing in anger. One is lost in a fantasy. Yet another anxiously fixates on the future while blaming the past. One part debates whether to answer the phone or let it ring just to keep listening to the song playing on the radio.

Now ask yourself, in the middle of all that, what chance does the voice of the Higher Self truly have to be heard?

You might think this example is exaggerated. Think again. That was you, driving home earlier. But do not feel bad; your friends are the same, if not worse, since they all have children, and you don't.

Author: Did you just make a sarcastic joke? Do Higher Selves do that?

Higher Self: Sure, why not?

(I laughed. At the same time, I felt an internal burst of joy coming from my Higher Self like a baby being tickled on both sides and unable to handle it. That is the closest description I can offer. At that time, I lost my meditative state, couldn't return to it, and had to prepare for work.)

****

Next day, after lunch, during meditation:

Author: Higher Self, you there?

Higher Self: I am always here with you and am particularly happy that we have now established yet another channel of communication.

Would you like to continue with our answer from yesterday?

Author: Yes, please.

Higher Self: So, what can you do when your mind becomes so overactive that it seems to silence the voice of your Higher Self?

The answer is Deep Conscious Harmonious Breathing.

What kind of breathing? Deep. Conscious. Harmonious.

Let me explain why this works. To breathe deeply and consciously, you must first bring your attention to the breath itself. That simple shift means you have already turned your focus away from everything else, especially the overthinking. Deeper breathing enhances brain oxygen flow, resulting in improved cognitive function.

Becoming conscious of your breath means noticing how air enters and leaves your body, and how each inhale and exhale affects different parts of you. As your awareness deepens, you begin to realize that your breathing is something you have control over. You can choose to breathe through your mouth, your nose, or both. You can take in a full breath or a shallow one. You begin to see that you have options.

Among all these options, you naturally choose what feels most harmonious to you. The traits of harmonious breathing are simple. It brings a natural smile to your face and causes no strain while you breathe. At the same time, you remain consciously aware of each breath, allowing it to be slightly deeper than usual.

And that's really the essence of this practice: to arrive at a place where you smile and just be. Once you have reached this state, stay with it for as long as you like. It is in this space that you can hear us clearly and begin to engage in a genuine conversation.

Additionally, make sure you choose a quiet spot. Turn off the radio and silence your phone. This practice can be performed with either open or closed eyes, while sitting or lying down, so choose whichever position feels most comfortable for you.

Now you have a new spiritual tool to incorporate during times when your mind becomes overactive, draining your energy, causing headaches, and interrupting your communication with your Higher Self. It is called Deep Conscious Harmonious Breathing.

Another lifestyle factor that contributes to creating an overwhelming mental chatter and ultimately makes it difficult to recognize our presence is the habit of constantly squeezing more things into our day. It is as if having free time is illegal, or the world might fall apart unless every moment is packed with activity. As a result, you are always rushing, and your body continuously releases cortisol. This stress hormone activates your fight-or-flight response, raises your heart rate, and keeps you on edge, which only fuels more overthinking.

So what can you do to break this cycle?

Start by admitting to yourself that you genuinely want and need more free time in your life. Go a step further and actually schedule it, block out short pockets of space in your day, even just twenty minutes here and there. Avoid overcommitting or saying yes to everything. Be more cautious when setting deadlines or making appointments. Add buffer time to them so that if something unexpected comes up, it will not throw you into panic or stress.

By creating more space in your life, your mind naturally becomes calmer and more receptive. It becomes much easier to hear your Higher Self when it is speaking to you.

Another group of pollutants worth mentioning, which can hinder communication with your Higher Self, are those that cloud mental clarity in any way. These include, but are not limited to, caffeine, nicotine, excessive sugar, alcohol, recreational drugs, and certain prescribed psychotropic medications.

We understand that some of these substances have become an integral part of your culture, but from our perspective, we have a very limited capacity for adaptation. (I discuss this further in Chapter 14.1.)

Author: Your advice and tips are great, but don't you have specific techniques that will ...

Higher Self: ... activate or connect you with your Higher Self?

(We both laughed)

Author: You are so me! I definitely will not go through the process of doing a Higher-Soul-ternity Test!

(We both laughed)

Higher Self: What kind of technique are you looking for, since there is nothing that needs to be activated or reconnected?

Author: A technique that makes your voice louder.

Higher Self: If you follow our advice and silence all the other sources of noise within you, you will hear us more clearly.

Author: I've heard there's a technique that makes the voice of the Higher Self sound in High Definition.

Higher Self: Oh, that one. Why didn't you say so?

(Author's Note: At that moment, I knew I was doomed! My biggest fear had come true. My Higher Self shared my devious, teasing attitude.)

Higher Self: Of course, we know exactly what you want. And most of the techniques are already familiar to you. Let's go over them.

First Technique: Deep Conscious Harmonious Breathing. Once you reach this state, you will be able to hear us clearly and engage in true conversation.

The second and third techniques could be those you use right after your meditation, when you rush to your computer to transcribe our conversation. You begin by saying, "Dear Higher Self, please help me remember as much of our conversation as possible." Then, start by recalling and writing down keywords and phrases in the order they were spoken. As you revisit each one, more details begin to flow. Before you know it, with our help, you have captured the full conversation and even more, since while transcribing, you usually ask new questions and receive their answers on the spot, and write them down too.

These two techniques can be used separately or in combination. Here they are clearly written out:

Second Technique: Calling us, acknowledging us, addressing us by name, and asking for our advice shows your desire to have a closer relationship with us, which we embrace.

Third Technique: Use something to write on. A notebook or your computer is fine. Start by calling on us and expressing what you would like to know. Then begin writing whatever thoughts or feelings come to mind about it. Say to yourself, "I feel this, but on the other hand, what if that happens?" Write down everything.

At some point, you will begin writing information that you have not thought about before, and that makes a lot of sense. It is clear and straightforward. That will be us.

This is also the answer to another question you may ask: "How can I distinguish which information comes from the Higher Self and which comes from other parts of us, such as our ego, emotions, or wishes?"

Our answers almost always make you go "ah." They make sense, are clear and straightforward, and come with warmth and comfort when needed. They are structured in such a way that they feel complete and resonate through all levels of your being.

The fourth technique offers a broad spectrum of benefits, making it valuable even for those who already communicate clearly with their Higher Self. Practicing this technique regularly will accelerate your spiritual journey by clearing energetic channels, awakening latent psychic abilities, and enhancing extrasensory awareness. In other words, the more you practice it, the more of your innate potential you will unlock.

This method combines visual, auditory, and energetic elements to activate specific energy centers and pathways within your energetic and etheric bodies. These areas are directly connected to your psychic abilities and your relationship with the Higher Self.

We refer to this as the **Opening of the 8th Gateway Technique**. But before we dive into the practice itself, we need to introduce you to the 8th main chakra, also known as the Higher Self Chakra. While you are already familiar with the chakra system and the Sushumna Nadi, like many others, you may not yet be aware of this higher energy center. Do not worry; the information is simple and easy to grasp.

(The Sushumna Nadi is the central vertical energy channel that connects all seven main chakras in the human body. It is considered the primary pathway for Kundalini energy to rise from the Root Chakra to the Crown Chakra. You can see its location in Appendix D)

All you need to know is that the Higher Self Chakra is located 6 to 7 inches (15 to 18 centimeters) above the crown of the head. It appears as an egg-shaped sphere of conscious energy, similar to the other chakras, measuring approximately 2 inches (5 centimeters) in diameter at birth and expanding up to 3 inches (8 centimeters) as your spiritual awareness develops, radiating a pure, etheric white light.

This energetic center is nourished and expanded by chanting the mantra **OM SHANTI OM**, a sound that reflects your harmonious alignment with divine presence and universal peace.

The 8th Gateway Technique:

Begin by sitting upright, either in a chair or on the floor in your preferred meditation posture, ensuring your spine is straight and relaxed.

Begin with **Deep Conscious Harmonious Breathing**, keeping your eyes closed.

Once you are centered, visualize your Higher Self Chakra located 6 to 7 inches (15 to 18 centimeters) above the crown of the head, glowing as a radiant, white, etheric sphere, about 3 inches in diameter.

Hold your attention there as you continue your Deep Conscious Harmonious Breathing.

Next, visualize, or better yet, sense yourself sitting at the center of a large four-sided energetic pyramid. This pyramid has no walls, only a glowing white radiating energy frame.

Now visualize a thick beam of brilliant light descending from above. It enters through the pyramid's apex through an opening, flows through your Higher Self Chakra, and continues downward all the way to the base of your Sushumna Nadi. The beam remains steady and unmoving throughout the meditation. The source of this light is your Over Soul, but if it feels more natural to see it coming from the Source of All That Is, the Universe, or any other divine origin, it is fine.

Take a few moments to feel the energy and structures you have activated.

Then affirm:

- **I am one with my Higher Self**
- **I am whole.**
- **I am one with all that is.**

Then chant the mantra **OM SHANTI OM** at least **13** times, feeling its vibration expand and strengthen the Higher Self Chakra and your entire energetic system.

When you finish, you have several options.

You may choose to rest in this state of deep meditative absorption, also known as **Samadhi** in yogic tradition. You can also use this heightened state to ask questions and receive answers intuitively, or use muscle testing to receive instant guidance from your selected Higher Source.

At times, you may notice or sense the pyramid structure beginning to rotate, either clockwise or counterclockwise. This movement is completely natural, and you should allow it to unfold without resistance. It simply reflects energetic shifts occurring within you, such as alignment, activation, or transformation.

- End of Session-

****

Wow! What an incredible gift to humanity the 8th Gateway Technique truly is. It is important to understand that this technique did not originate solely from my Higher Self, but from the Higher Self we all share. It was given to us with a divine purpose. Since connecting deeply with my Higher Self, it has become my most trusted companion, teacher, life coach, and ascension coach. You can absolutely experience this too. All it takes is a little dedication and sincere commitment. Keep going and stay engaged with this book. You are almost there, and what awaits you is truly life-changing.

****

The fact that your Higher Self holds your soul's blueprint, the records of all your lifetimes and experiences, including those between incarnations, and maintains direct access to your Over Soul makes the Higher Self a Higher Source of Knowledge and Wisdom.

By connecting to your Higher Self, you can uncover insights and answers to questions such as:

- Your spiritual growth, life purpose, and path.
- Determining which aspects of your life need adjustment to align with your true purpose.
- Soul contracts affecting specific areas of your life.
- Perspectives on God and religion.

- Insights into past lives.
- Optimal directions for personal and professional decisions.
- Understanding life-changing events and their reasons.
- Identifying the right mentors for guidance.
- Awakening psychic abilities and opening chakras.
- Inviting additional inner guides for specific assistance.
- Interpreting dreams.
- Timing and strategies for pursuing dreams and removing obstacles.

P.S.: The Higher Self is one of the three Higher Sources of Knowledge and Wisdom, which, due to the sensitive information it holds, is governed by specific terms and conditions. This means you must first ask whether you are permitted to access the information you are seeking. To avoid having to ask twice, I recommend including "Cannot answer" as one of your possible response options. I find this very convenient.

Question: "Why did following my Higher Self's guidance resulted in what seemed like a negative outcome?"

Answer: The guidance will always align with lessons that foster long-term spiritual growth, even if your Lower Self perceives some experiences as negative or catastrophic.

The truth is that all experiences, regardless of how they are classified, are integral to growth and spiritual ascension. Unlike other Higher Sources of Knowledge and Wisdom, the Higher Self is the only one that provides answers while considering many factors, such as the blueprint of your soul's journey, your soul's goals for this lifetime, karma, and your various soul contracts.

10.5. Angels and Archangels

Across cultures and religions, Angels and Archangels are revered for their deep love, devotion, and closeness to God. They embody purity and wisdom and are often depicted as luminous beings of pure light and energy. Their role in relation to humans is believed to be that of divine messengers and guides, assisting individuals on their spiritual journeys. Their sacred purpose and celestial nature make them a powerful source of Higher Knowledge and Wisdom, especially in matters of the Divine.

However, my personal experiences with communicating, interacting, and even trance-channeling two Archangels were disappointing. I prefer not to disclose their names, but they are among the four most well-known ones. While I initially felt betrayed, disillusioned, and that I had wasted my time, I now understand that, like all seemingly negative experiences, it served a purpose. Every life challenge is ultimately a lesson designed to push us further along our spiritual path. In my case, these interactions led me to seek guidance from two Sources of Higher Knowledge and Wisdom, where I learned the truth about the nature of Angels and Archangels for the first time.

My intention in sharing these experiences is not to negatively influence your perception or future interactions with them but rather to offer a more comprehensive perspective to my readers.

Omitting my experiences would feel like a disservice, perpetuating the traditional narratives about Angels that may leave others unprepared or disappointed, as I was. It's important to remember that the insights shared in this book are not absolute or mandated. Ultimately, there is no obligation to accept or apply whatever is written here. You always have free choice in everything you do. At the end of the day, you hold autonomy over every aspect of your life and spiritual journey.

My Experiences with Angels

Between 2016 and 2018, I participated in online channeling classes with a UK-based teacher who prefers to remain anonymous. During these sessions, my teacher guided me into a trance state, allowing a spirit to communicate through me.

From the very beginning, an Archangel entered my energy field. To be honest, I had been hoping for an extraterrestrial, given my fascination with them. My teacher spent an hour asking the Archangel various questions on topics such as the Angelic hierarchy, their duties, the nature of love, whether animals have souls, and much more.

The answers provided by the Archangel were remarkable in their clarity, originality, and depth. I felt deeply honored to be in the presence of such an extraordinary being.

Months later, during one of our private interactions, while meditating, I asked if he would be willing to channel his healing energies through me to help others. He liked the idea and agreed. I then suggested using me as a case study to explore what an entire healing session would look and feel like from beginning to end. He thought it was a great idea, so I described two health issues I was experiencing. He provided a detailed analysis of how and why these issues had developed and offered advice on actions I could take to support the healing process.

He then advised me to relax and be open and receptive to his healing energies. During the first healing session, I felt noticeable energy currents throughout my body. It was an exhilarating experience that left me feeling hopeful.

Our subsequent sessions began with addressing my general questions about healing, followed by a healing session for me. While I could feel the energies during these sessions, I noticed that my symptoms persisted, and I was not experiencing any real improvement.

Frustrated, I asked why there were no results despite feeling his energies, and each time, I was given a different explanation for why the healing was not manifesting.

As months passed, my frustration grew. One day, I decided to confront him, intending to question his effectiveness. I planned to say, "Listen, you are a 12th-dimensional Archangel. You explained the causes of my issues and how correcting my attitude was supposed to help. I have learned my lesson and received your healing energies several times, yet my condition remains unchanged, and each time you offer a different excuse." However, on the day I planned to confront him, he stopped attending during my meditation time.

A similar situation unfolded with a second Archangel I had invited during meditation, leading to the same outcome.

Both experiences understandably left me upset and disappointed. Determined to gain clarity and avoid such situations in the future, I turned to my Higher Self for guidance.

Comments from My Higher Self About My Experiences with the Two Angels:

Understanding some fundamental truths about the nature of angels and the plane of existence you currently inhabit will make this topic much easier to grasp.

Let's begin by defining some of the primary roles of angels, which involve tasks of immense cosmic significance. They maintain creation, safeguard divine order, and facilitate spiritual evolution across dimensions.

Maintaining creation and safeguarding divine order are the most profound among their responsibilities, as no other entity in the universe holds such immense power over creation outside the Source of Creation itself. For example, if a massive comet were on a collision course with a planet, whether inhabited or not, angels would intervene if that impact was not meant to occur. If multiple nuclear bombs were on the verge of detonating on Earth, triggering a chain reaction that could destroy the planet, angels would step in to prevent it, but only if it was not meant to happen.

When events of great magnitude threaten to unfold outside of divine timing, direct angelic intervention ensures that they do not occur. The opposite is also true, as certain events are facilitated to ensure they occur at the right time. Their ways of making these reality course corrections are limitless, always working unseen to maintain balance.

On a smaller scale, similar deviations can occur in an individual's life. The Higher Self and the Over Soul, both of which have an intimate understanding of a person's soul contract, continuously monitor their experiences and lessons, working to bring the right situations and encounters into their life. However, very few people beyond the age of seven manage to fulfil everything outlined in their soul contract for a given lifetime.

This is because, as we have expressed many times to you, you are not alone on this planet. Every individual shares their journey with countless others, especially in their vicinity, and each person has their own soul contracts to fulfil. As a result, circumstances often arise that may lead a person away from experiencing their intended path. In some cases, neither the Higher Self nor the Over Soul can directly intervene in a way that will realign that person with their soul contract or soul plan. It is in these situations that the Higher Self turns to the angelic realm for assistance. In response, an angel will step in and intervene to realign the individual's journey with their intended soul plan. From this perspective, angels are everywhere, continuously engaged with humanity. They always respond when called upon by an individual's Higher Self. However, the response is often quite different when humans directly request something from an angel or archangel.

In many of our discussions, we have compared Earth to a vast school, a place where souls come to learn and grow through experience. Just as students in a school are guided by teachers suited to their level, so too are Inner Guides assigned based on a soul's stage of development and specific needs.

When we say that angels facilitate spiritual evolution across dimensions, it is essential to understand that they primarily serve as master teachers and supervisors. They are assigned only to students nearing the end of their journey, souls on the verge of graduation.

For humans, this occurs when ascending to the sixth dimension. At that stage, you have undergone countless lessons, gained profound wisdom, and evolved energetically and spiritually to the point where you have shed your physical body.

Even within this dimension, angels will not engage with you unless you have reached at least level six, often referred to as the sixth density. Each dimension consists of thirteen levels, with the twelfth being the final stage before ascension and the thirteenth representing the culmination of all previous wisdom and experiences carried into the next higher dimension.

This means that angels rarely intervene in the lives of individual souls who have not yet reached the sixth dimension and surpassed level six. Below this stage, souls are guided by other teachers and supervisors better suited to their development, such as spirit guides, the Higher Self, and the Over Soul.

This means that true angels will rarely step forward to respond to requests from individual souls living in the fifth and sixth dimensions. While there are exceptions, these are determined by the Higher Self. Angelic interactions always align perfectly with the divine plan, divine timing, and the soul contracts of both individuals and collectives.

To address the inevitable question of who responds to these angelic requests when asked by humans coming from these lower levels, then we would say that the answer could come from a number of sources. For example, it could come from your subconscious mind, one of your inner guides, or your Higher Self, and so on.

However, depending on the circumstances, such as the state of the different bodies (mental, etheric, emotional, energetic), timing, and the environment or circumstances we are in at the moment of request, an individual can also attract a low-level spirit or a high-level spirit to come close to them to impersonate an Angel or Archangel and even God to answer that question on their behalf. That answer can come in many forms, such as a thought, a voice speaking to you within, a thought, an image, a feeling, an instant understanding or realization, intuition, and so on. It can also be facilitated through the use of a divination tool, such as a pendulum or self-muscle testing.

I will now elaborate on the scenario in which a spirit impersonates an angel and responds to your calling. This situation carries specific ramifications compared to the other sources we have discussed.

The type of spirit that responds is determined by the vibrational state of the person making the request. If the individual is joyful, filled with positive emotions, and living in a high-vibrational state with strong and balanced etheric and energetic bodies, they will attract a high-level spirit impersonating an angel, as is the case with you.

Conversely, someone sad, disheartened, or overwhelmed by negative emotions and living in a low-vibrational state with weak and unbalanced etheric and energetic bodies will attract low-level spirits.

However, there are exceptions, even for those in the first group. For example, a person with high vibrations who faces a challenging situation, such as coping with a loved one's severe illness, and spends time in hospitals or other environments that may drain or disrupt their energetic and etheric bodies, could attract a low-level spirit impersonating an angel. In such situations, these low-level spirits might infiltrate their auric field and other layers of their energetic composition.

Low-level spirits impersonating angels can cause harm. Once they respond to a call, they may choose to remain within the auric field and energy body, feeding off the individual's energy. This is known as a spirit possession. While it may not be as dramatic as depictions in horror movies like The Exorcist, it involves the unwanted presence of a low-level entity within someone's energy field.

These spirits impersonating Angels or Archangels often make unfulfilled promises, leading individuals already in a low vibratory state further into despair, mental illness, and, in extreme cases, even suicide."

High-level spirits impersonating angels typically have good intentions. They are advanced spirits who choose to impersonate angels in order to prevent the disappointment that might result from an unanswered call. These spirits often act as 'special' guides, stepping in when someone's Higher Self requests additional spiritual help for their Lower Self (the aspect of us living on Earth). Their teachings and consultations are of high quality.

Nevertheless, they are not angels whom the person initially called upon. High-level spirits impersonating angels do not linger in a person's aura unless requested. They offer love, understanding, and guidance without causing harm, though their failure to fulfil promises can sometimes lead to frustration.

Generally speaking, an answer is always provided instantly whenever you ask a question. However, since the response often originates beyond the physical dimension, you need activated psychic centers to perceive it. Some individuals have their psychic centers completely deactivated or blocked, relying solely on logical reasoning to find answers. Others have their psychic centers partially or moderately opened or activated, allowing them to receive answers through intuition, a hunch, or other subtle forms, depending on which psychic abilities, or "clairs," are partially or moderately active. Finally, those with fully opened and activated psychic centers can consciously perceive the complete answer provided to them.

Author: Hold on, I am shocked. Are you saying that spirits impersonate angels to such an extent that they can drive someone to commit suicide, and angels allow this?

Higher Self: For this dimension, the answer is yes. As you may have realized by now, Earth's schooling system is designed to offer a full spectrum of experiences, including lessons in deception. Paradoxically, while Earth is highly regulated, anything still goes. There are countless rules, terms, and conditions shaping the nature of experience here, yet one of the fundamental principles is that anything is possible.

These structures exist to ensure that souls can access the experiences they seek without needing to search for them in another plane of existence, which could complicate and delay their soul journey. In such cases, your Higher Self requests from the angelic realm to remove a spirit impersonating an angel at the appropriate moment or to allow its presence with or without conditions. This decision is made primarily based on the individual's soul contract.

****

In a separate meditation session, I connected with the Akashic Records to gain a deeper understanding of this phenomenon or perhaps to explore a different perspective. I am including this response here because I believe it provides a valuable opportunity for you to observe how two distinct Higher Sources of Knowledge and Wisdom convey their answers, including the differences in tone and structure.

Question: Dear Guardian of the Akashic Records (also known as librarians), I am seeking to understand why 12th-dimensional Angels and Archangels may choose not to interact with humans when called upon, and why they allow other spirits to impersonate them as angels.

Answer: "Certainly, one moment, please."
(My body was subtly adjusted to improve communication.)

Let us begin by examining the fundamental nature and role of angels within the cosmic order. Contrary to popular belief, the angelic realm does not have an inherent hierarchy. All angels exist on the same level of authority, functioning as unified expressions of divine intelligence.

The notion of an angelic hierarchy originated from a monk who, seeking divine guidance, prayed for insight into the roles and structure of angels. In response, a high-level spirit imparted knowledge about their function and subsequently framed this information within a hierarchical structure, complete with a male characterization.

This interpretation reflected the spiritual and cultural perspectives of that era rather than the true nature of angels.

Angels don’t have genders, nor do they embody dominant masculine or feminine energies. However, as omnipotent beings, they can manifest in any form or density they choose.

Their consciousness is collective, meaning each angel operates in perfect unity, thinking and acting as a singular, harmonious force within the divine framework.

No entity outside the Source of Creation itself holds comparable authority over the fabric of existence.

Their primary responsibilities include maintaining creation, safeguarding divine order, and overseeing spiritual evolution across countless dimensions.

Earth serves as an advanced training ground for souls, complete with its own existential goals, laws, and conditions. Angels safeguard these principles, ensuring they remain upheld and unbroken.

Angels honor the mortal experience by upholding the principle that humans must navigate their own journey, make their own decisions, overcome challenges, and uncover their true nature through personal effort.

Life on Earth as a fourth-density, fourth-dimension being is among the most challenging of all, as Earth's experiential system accommodates all possibilities within its structured learning framework.

In this dimension, encounters with entities impersonating angels, whether guided by benevolent or malignant intent, are considered legitimate challenges. These experiences are intentionally included as part of the soul’s journey before ascending to the next level.

The allowance or removal of such spirit impersonators is not arbitrary but is governed by the Higher Self in accordance with the individual’s soul contract. Within this framework, the Higher Self determines the extent to which external influences are permitted, ensuring that each experience aligns with the soul’s intended evolution.

****

I hope you found the answers from these two different Higher Sources of Knowledge and Wisdom thought-provoking and enjoyable. At the very least, I hope they offered valuable insights into this fascinating topic.

Regardless of my personal experiences and additional information, you can always choose to connect with a specific Angel or the Angelic collective if your heart desires.

You can expect to uncover insights and answers to questions such as:

1. How can I improve my understanding and connection with the divine?
2. How can I align more closely with my spiritual path?
3. What is my life purpose?
4. How can I best serve as a source of light and love for those around me?
5. What practices will help me strengthen my connection with my guardian Angel?
6. What is the most important message you have for me at this stage of my journey?
7. How can I release fear and embrace unconditional love?
8. What lessons am I meant to learn from my current life challenges?
9. How can I effectively heal from past traumas and move forward?
10. How can I contribute to the healing and betterment of the world?
11. In what ways can I develop my spiritual gifts?
12. What steps should I take to cultivate inner peace and harmony?

P.S.: Personally, if I had such pressing questions and sought answers, knowing what I now know about angels, I would choose to connect with my Higher Self to find those answers.

PPS: Please do not assume that I look down on angels in any way. I simply understand their true nature and, for that reason, choose not to contact them directly. If anything, I would ask my Higher Self to convey a message on my behalf.

Well-known Angels/Archangels include: Michael, Raphael, Uriel, Gabriel, Metatron, Sandalphon, Ariel, Raziel, Cassiel, Zadkiel, Raguel, Camael, Jophiel, and Jeremiel.

To sum up:

- The belief that every Angelic encounter involves an angel is a misconception. Both higher and lower-level spirits can impersonate angels.
- True angelic messages always promote peace, love, and spiritual growth.
- True angelic presence is typically transient and not permanent, differing from those of your personal spirit guides and lower-level spirits.
- Angels rarely interact with humans in the fourth and fifth dimensions.
- If healing is offered, it will be profound and undeniable, not temporary or dubious.

****

10.6. **Akashic Records (AKA - Universal Mind)**

The Akashic Records are the most comprehensive database of all Higher Sources of Knowledge and Wisdom that exist, yet they function as a singular consciousness. They are often described as a universal repository containing the history of all creation.

According to ancient Hindu philosophy and Theosophy, the Akashic Records serve as the repository where the history of all creation is recorded and stored. The term 'Akashic' originates from the Sanskrit word 'Akasha,' meaning 'Sky.' In Hindu philosophy, Akasha is considered the first element of creation, formed in the astral plane, followed by Air, Fire, Water, and Earth, collectively known as Pancha-mahabhuta or "the five supreme powers."

Being the subtlest and most expansive element, Akasha extends from the astral to the physical plane, creating a medium known as the Akashic medium, where both material and non-material elements coexist. Unlike the other four elements, which are dynamic and constantly changing as they embody the essence of everything in our world, the Akashic medium remains permanently static.

The Akashic Records can be envisioned as the master records of the cosmos, encompassing the history and the ever-changing potential futures of all existence. For humans, every action, intent, word, feeling, thought, belief system, event, sound, and experience that has occurred in all planes of existence since the beginning of creation is imprinted and recorded in the Akashic medium.

The concept of the Akashic medium traces its origins to the Vedic Civilization, also known as the Indus Valley Civilization, which flourished in what is now the Indian subcontinent. This civilization is considered the birthplace of Hindu thought, philosophy, spirituality, cosmology, and science.

The earliest references to the Akashic medium can be found in the Vedic texts, some of the oldest sacred writings known to humanity, which were composed over centuries, with some dating back as far as 1500 BC.

A deeper philosophical exploration of Akasha and its connection to consciousness becomes clearer in later texts, such as the Upanishads, written between 800 and 400 BC, and the Brahma Sutras, composed around 300 to 400 AD.

Although rarely acknowledged, it is an undeniable truth that modern Western science often takes concepts and knowledge that were well known and understood thousands of years ago by ancient civilizations, rebrands them, presents them as groundbreaking discoveries, and claims credit for them. The Akashic medium is no exception. Modern Western science has introduced various terms to describe it, such as the Quantum Field, Unified Field, Zero-Point Field, Collective Unconscious, Holographic Universe, Information Field, Mind Field, and Consciousness Field.

****

Now, here is some fascinating information about the Akashic Records that no one talks about and that I have personally accessed!

The Akashic Records exist in both material and non-material forms. In their material form, they are stored on the surface of select stars, with only three or four per universe, each uniquely designed to safeguard this sacred knowledge. For ultimate security and preservation, one of these stars remains forever hidden, beyond the reach of anyone, ensuring the eternal survival of the cosmic archives. These stars are adorned with countless individual crystals, each encoding the history of a planet, star, and other structures, entities, and events.

For instance, you would find several crystals grouped together if you were seeking to explore the history of our solar system's planets.

Access to the material Akashic Records is limited to technologically advanced civilizations with spaceships or teleportation abilities, subject to permission from the 'Head Librarian'—the star's consciousness or a 10th-dimensional collective being. Numerous 'ordinary' librarians, typically 5th- and 6th-dimensional beings, are stationed there to assist visitors in finding what they are looking for and maintain and protect these records.

Due to their remote physical location, not everyone can access the material Akashic Records, which is why they are also available in a non-material dimension, making them more accessible to a broader range of beings.

By connecting to the Akashic Records, you can uncover insights and answers to just about anything! You can explore the universe's history, past, present, and future possible timelines. You can unravel the answers to mysteries that have long puzzled humankind and discover truths about yourself and others. As the most extensive library in existence, it provides a unique and enriching opportunity for learning and self-discovery.

Question: Why explore other Higher Sources of Knowledge and Wisdom if the Akashic Records contain all answers?

There are two main reasons:

1. Accessing the Akashic Records can sometimes be challenging. Like other Higher Sources of Knowledge and Wisdom, they are governed by specific rules and guidelines, which you may unknowingly violate, preventing you from receiving the information you seek.

   Additionally, some individuals find it difficult to establish a clear connection with the Akashic Records. This is completely normal. In practice, you will notice that the energy and connection with certain Higher Sources come more naturally than with others. In most cases, adopting the Extensive Self-Muscle Testing Approach will significantly enhance your ability to connect with any Higher Source. Chapter 14 provides detailed explanations of the three different approaches for accessing these sources.

2. Lack of Personal Connection. Unlike other sources such as your Inner Guides, Higher Self, 6th-dimensional self, and Over Soul, the Akashic Records lack emotions, personality, and individuality. Some individuals do not mind this and even prefer it, while others find it unappealing. Ultimately, it all comes down to personal preference.

Akashic Records - Rules and Guidelines:

When accessing the Akashic Records, be aware that certain data may be restricted or inaccessible. Instances include:

- Interference with Soul Contracts: Access may be blocked if it negatively impacts your own or someone else's soul contract.
- Information About Others: Accessing records of living individuals requires their direct permission or that of their Higher Self.
- Intentions: Access will be denied if the information could potentially harm an individual or entity.
- Discretion of the guardians: There might be undisclosed reasons known only to the guardians (librarians) of the Akashic Records.

What the Akashic Records Are Not:

The Akashic Records are not a place to receive healing energies of any kind. They have no direct influence on your life; their effect depends entirely on how you choose to use the information you are given. They also do not provide opinions. However, if you phrase your questions and list of options wisely, you will know which option is the best for you. A detailed example is provided in Chapter 12.

REMEMBER!

Even when using the Extensive Approach to access the Akashic Records, which increases the success rate of connecting to any of the Higher Sources of Knowledge and Wisdom, it is essential always to begin using self-muscle testing to confirm whether you have gained access or not. Don't just assume you have entered it.

There is another factor to consider as well. The Akashic Records is one of the three Higher Sources of Knowledge and Wisdom, which, due to the sensitive information they hold, are governed by specific terms and conditions.

This means you must first ask whether you are permitted to access the information you are seeking. To avoid having to ask twice, I recommend including "Cannot answer" as one of your possible response options. I find this very convenient.

After your session, you may choose to access another Higher Source of Knowledge and Wisdom to receive answers to the questions that the Akashic Records declined to answer.

> ***"You carry the blueprint of the universe within you. When you trust your inner knowing, you align with cosmic wisdom and embody your soul's purpose."***
>
> *— George C. Georgiou*

CHAPTER 11

Well-known Higher Sources of Knowledge and Wisdom with Collective Consciousness:

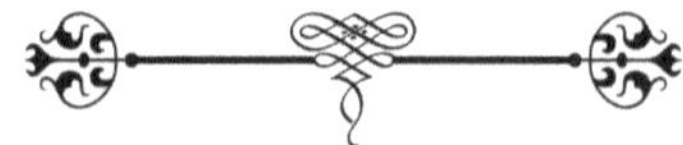

11.1. Over Soul
11.2. Mother Earth
11.3. Infinite more

11.1. Over Soul Collective

In the grand, intricate life of a Creator such as you, me, and everyone else, when creators venture out from the Source of Creation to explore and experience their creations, they do so in groups, or, more precisely, in teams. It is one of the mechanisms created to ensure that each soul has the proper tools and support to complete the creator's journey successfully.

So why was there a need for a team? The following acronym captures the essence of a true team and reveals its ultimate purpose: TEAM, which stands for Together Everyone Achieves More.

Each Oversoul is a collective consciousness composed of 144,000 individual souls, or team members. What is essential to understand is that the Oversoul represents a consciousness vastly greater than that of your Higher Self. Positioned vibrationally above the Higher Self, it resides even closer to the Source of Creation. If the Higher Self aligns with the seventh dimension and density, the Oversoul corresponds with the eighth, existing as a collective energy of immense power.

These 144,000 individual souls that comprise one Oversoul share a profound connection and carry identical vibrational frequencies. That is why when two such souls happen to meet randomly, an instant and often 'unexplainable' emotional connection is felt between them, accompanied by the feeling of Deja Vu.

Both of those feelings are justifiable as they most likely met in one or more past/future lifetimes, exchanged experiences, and created karma between them, further complicating their connection as seen from a human perspective.

Of course, once you pass on and leave the Earthly plane, during the time between lifetimes, when you are able to access additional information about the events that took place in your lifetime, information that you couldn't know at the time, then everything makes sense and you find yourself relieved that, regardless of your experiences, you have progressed on your soul journey.

It is in the Oversoul plane of existence that a soul comes when seeking to experience something specific and looks for one or more souls to participate and assist in achieving this. Here, there are always plenty of volunteers who are eager to help and willing to take on the necessary roles. "This is the very essence of the Oversoul, where each team member collaborates and supports one another on their shared journey". That was the final remark of my sixth-dimensional self, who was educating me on the topic.

****

Feedback from my workshop participants has revealed that receiving answers from the Oversoul is often considered the most challenging compared to other Higher Sources of Knowledge and Wisdom. This challenge usually stems from an emotional component. They would commonly say, "I received an answer, but I am not sure if it came from my Oversoul or if my own desires and expectations influenced the response." In other words, they struggle with the possibility of receiving a false positive or false negative answer during self-muscle testing.

In truth, this challenge can arise with any Higher Source of Knowledge and Wisdom. To receive a clear and unbiased answer, it is essential to approach the process from a neutral state, free from emotions and expectations about the desired outcome. Of course, achieving this level of neutrality is easier said than done. If connecting with the Oversoul proves difficult for any reason, I suggest switching to your Higher Self. Any questions intended for the Oversoul can just as easily be directed to the Higher Self, which can retrieve the answers for you effortlessly.

When connecting with your Oversoul collective, you can expect to uncover valuable insights and answers to questions such as:

- Does this person belong to the same Oversoul as I do?
- Could this person be my soulmate?

Regardless of the answer, you can always choose to explore further and discover meaningful insights about your future or existing partner on a spiritual level. You might ask:

- Did we share past lives together? How many lifetimes did we share? Where and when did these occur?
- What karmic agreements or experiences bind us together in this lifetime?
- What key qualities or virtues must I cultivate to fulfill my soul's purpose in this lifetime?
- What past life experiences are most relevant to my current challenges or relationships, and how can I integrate those lessons now?
- What is the significance of the people and experiences in my life, and how do they contribute to my soul's growth?

P.S.: The Over Soul is one of the three Higher Sources of Knowledge and Wisdom, which, due to the sensitive information it holds, is governed by specific terms and conditions. This means you must first ask whether you are

permitted to access the information you are seeking. To avoid having to ask twice, I recommend including "Cannot answer" as one of your possible response options. I find this very convenient.

11.2. Mother Earth/Gaia

Mother Earth, also known as Gaia, is a vast 10th-dimensional living organism infused with immense consciousness. While it possesses a singular awareness, it also holds countless individual and collective energetic imprints that can be accessed instantly to provide the answers we seek. Within her field of existence, you can find energetic imprints of the Plant Kingdom, the Animal Kingdom, the Atlantean Collective, and many others. These imprints serve as reservoirs of knowledge, making Gaia similar in function to the Akashic Records.

Gaia's existence spans billions of years, acting as a vast archive that records every event on and beneath her surface, as well as within the atmosphere. Through Gaia, you can access knowledge about the entire universe, as she is connected to the cosmos through an intricate network of etheric grid systems. She is also linked to at least one star or planet that holds the Akashic Records in physical form.

By connecting with Mother Earth, you can uncover insights and answers to questions such as:

- The history of Earth and the rise and fall of various civilizations
- The evolutionary journey of humans and other species
- Archaeological mysteries and Earth's ancient secrets
- The nature and dynamics of Earth's energies and substances
- The history of interactions between Earth and extraterrestrial civilizations and beings
- Earth's relationships with the moon, other planets, and the broader solar system

11.3. Infinite More

In this book, I have elaborated on eight Higher Sources of Knowledge and Wisdom that I consider the most significant and widely accessible. Due to their scope and relevance, I believe they are well-suited to meet the needs of the general population. However, these are by no means the only ones. In reality, there are infinitely more, particularly among those with a collective consciousness. Those with a singular consciousness can generally be found within the Akashic Records, so to speak, under one roof.

On the other hand, those with a collective consciousness can be accessed within the Akashic Records but may also be directly accessed as independent sources.

To refresh your memory, a collective consciousness refers to a unified consciousness shared by a group or population, bound together by common origins, experiences, values, traditions, or stages of evolution. Below is a small selection of additional Sources of Knowledge and Wisdom with collective consciousness, provided as examples, that you can directly access to gain insights and information:

- The Fairies Collective
- The Nature Spirits and Deities Collective
- The Atlanteans Collective
- The Lemurians Collective
- The Sumerian Civilization Collective
- The Indus Valley Civilization Collective
- The Ancient Greeks Collective
- The Ancient Egyptians Collective
- The Ancient Romans Collective
- The Ancient Druids Collective

- The Ancient Arcturian Collective
- The Modern Arcturian Collective
- The Ancient Pleiadian Collective
- The Modern Pleiadian Collective
- The Milky Way Collective
- The Solar System Collective

These collectives function similarly to any of the main Higher Sources of Knowledge and Wisdom. For example, let's consider **the Fairies Collective**. This source holds the energetic imprint of the fairy kingdom's history, knowledge, and wisdom. Engaging with this collective can provide profound insights into questions related explicitly to fairies.

When connecting with the Fairies Collective, you can expect to uncover valuable insights and answers to questions such as:

- Is there a fairy living in the forest near my home?
- Would this fairy be open to friendship?
- Where is the best place for us to meet?
- How can I respectfully communicate and build trust with fairies?
- Are there specific offerings or gestures that fairies appreciate?
- What role do fairies play in maintaining balance in nature?
- Have I had any past-life connections or experiences with the fairy realm?

Final Remark:

*If you are uncertain about the existence of a particular collective, you can always inquire about it within the Akashic Records.

CHAPTER 12

How to Formulate Questions for Accurate and Insightful Self-Muscle Testing

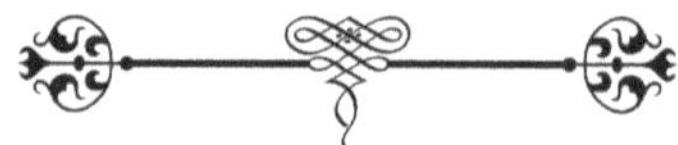

One limitation of self-muscle testing as a divination method is that it provides only a strong or weak muscle response, translating to a 'Yes' or 'No' or a 'True' or 'False' answer. However, by carefully formulating our questions, we can overcome this limitation and obtain more detailed and insightful responses.

In general, there are two types of questions: open-ended and closed-ended.

Open-ended Questions

Open-ended questions encourage more detailed responses. They typically begin with:

- How...?
- In what way...?
- Could you explain...?
- Could you please analyze...?
- Can you elaborate on...?
- Could you summarize...?
- Could you describe...?

While open questions are very helpful, they are only effective when addressed to a Higher Source of Knowledge and Wisdom if you have developed at least one extra-sensory perception (ESP). In other words, if you are a psychic or medium, you may be able to perceive the detailed answer given to you.

If you are reading this book, I'm guessing that you have not yet reached that level, just like I hadn't years ago. The good news is that with consistent self-muscle testing practice, especially when using the Extensive Self-Muscle Testing Approach and following my advice in the 'About the Author' section, you can start developing your psychic abilities within just a couple of months.

Since you are not a psychic yet, we will avoid using open-ended questions for now. Instead, there is a clever alternative that is almost as effective.

<u>Closed-ended Questions</u>

Closed-ended questions are designed to elicit a short, specific answer, usually 'Yes' or 'No,' or 'True' or 'False.'

Here are some examples:

- Do you ...?
- Did you ...?
- Will the ...?
- Would you ...?
- What day of the week ...?
- What color is the ...?

When using self-muscle testing as a divination tool, we rely on closed-ended and multiple-choice questions to obtain our answers.

Here is a fun example of a closed-ended question:
"Should I buy the red pair of shoes or the yellow ones?" Yes or No? 😊

Multiple-Choice Questions

Multiple-choice questions are a type of closed-ended question that helps us move beyond the simple 'Yes' or 'No' format. This is the clever alternative I mentioned earlier.

By using multiple-choice questions, we ask the Higher Source of Knowledge and Wisdom to indicate the best option from a set of possibilities we have prepared.

Examples of Prepared Questions:

Dear Inner Guide, which option would you recommend as the best choice for me at this moment?

- Option 1: Is going to ... and ... the best option for me?
- Option 2: Would canceling my trip to ... be the best option for me?
- Option 3: Would changing my plans to ... be the best option?
- Option 4: None of the above is the best option, and I should continue searching for alternatives.

You then proceed to test each option individually using self-muscle testing to receive a 'Yes' or 'No' response.

Here is another example:

Dear Over Soul, under these circumstances and at this particular moment in my life, would it be wise for me to:

a. Option 1

b. Option 2

c. Option 3

d. Do nothing for now

e. None of the above (indicating there is a better option not listed)

f. Cannot answer

Please note how the above example utilizes the Over Soul as its Higher Source of Knowledge and Wisdom, and just like in the case of the Akashic Records, includes the option 'Cannot answer'.

I find closed and multiple-choice questions very effective because their answers are always transparent and straightforward. They also help clarify insights gained through extra-sensory perception. For example, while meditating and asking a question, I might see an image with an inner voice commenting (clairaudience), making the message easy to understand. However, sometimes I receive an image or impressions that are unclear or open to interpretation. In these cases, I use self-muscle testing to verify whether my understanding of it is correct.

Special Considerations Regarding the Akashic Records:

Since the Akashic Records do not provide opinions of any kind, you can get around this by cleverly phrasing your question and list of options. For example, for a personal question, you might phrase it like this:

Akashic Records, if I do this...(list your intent)..., the most likely outcome will be:

a. Positive and pleasant
b. Negative and unpleasant

I wouldn't suggest using the following wording:

a) Positive
b) Negative

For example, you might receive an answer saying 'positive' and decide to go ahead, only to have a negative experience. It happened to me at least twice, which caused me trouble and disappointment. But I learned my lesson and I want to share it with you so you can avoid it. The reason why the Akashic Records indicate an option that leads to a negative outcome or situation has to do with two reasons: one you can control and one you cannot. The first reason relates to how the Akashic Records perceive Positive and Negative, and similarly, how you perceive what is positive and negative.

Let me explain. If that negative outcome or experience teaches you something valuable that benefits you for the rest of your life, and it was even one of the experiences you chose for your current life — in other words, you checked off an item from your soul contract for this lifetime — then would you say that experience was negative or positive? This issue can be avoided if you phrase your answer in a more accurate way:

a) Positive and pleasant or b) Negative and unpleasant.

Having said that, you can always choose to be brave and adventurous and stick with the simple positive–negative answers!

The second reason why you might receive an answer saying 'Positive' or even 'Positive and pleasant' and decide to go ahead, only to have a negative experience, relates to the fact that one or more events occurred that caused the expected outcome to change. Remember, we are not living on this planet alone; we share it with billions of other people, each concerned about their path and agenda, and their paths can unexpectedly cross yours.

Generally, by skillfully crafting multiple-choice questions about the topic, you unlock the full potential of self-muscle testing, making it a precise and dependable guidance tool.

"Once you make a decision, the universe conspires to make it happen."

—Ralph Waldo Emerson

CHAPTER 13

Mastering Self-Muscle Testing Techniques for Multidimensional Divination

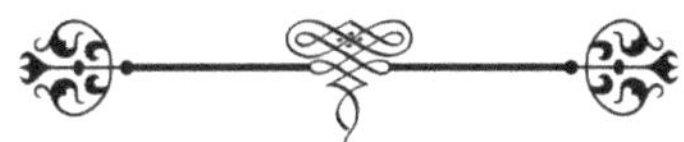

1. **Whole-arm test technique**
2. **Single-loop test technique**
3. **Double-loop test technique**
4. **Fingers-wedge test technique**
5. **Thumb-pinky loop technique**
6. **Flexed-elbow test technique**
7. **Scissor-fingers test technique**
8. **The finger-on-finger test technique**

13.1 Preparing for Your Self-Muscle Testing Journey

I appreciate your patience and congratulate you on reaching this stage. I know many of you were eager to dive straight into learning self-muscle testing techniques. However, as with anything in life, building a strong foundation is essential before moving forward.

What is the point of learning self-muscle testing if you do not fully understand what it is, its history, the various Higher Sources of Knowledge and Wisdom available, which source is most appropriate to consult based on your inquiry, or how to properly formulate your questions to receive the best possible answers? The previous sections provided the essential knowledge you need to use self-muscle testing as a multidimensional divination tool confidently.

Now, I will guide you step by step through eight different self-muscle testing techniques. You might wonder if it is possible to learn these techniques without a video demonstration. The answer is yes. I have simplified everything, providing clear instructions, accurate information, and helpful images to make learning easy and effective.

That being said, I encourage you to visit YouTube, the world's largest online video library, and watch up to three videos that demonstrate self-muscle testing techniques. This will give you a general idea of what we aim to accomplish. If you choose to do this, go to the website, type **"how to muscle test yourself"** in the search bar, and press Enter. Be sure to select videos that are at least three minutes long, as shorter ones may not be suitable. Additionally, avoid watching more than three, as this could interfere with your learning process.

I have personally reviewed many videos on this topic, and none explain the technique as thoroughly as I do in the following sections.

Before you begin practicing, find a quiet space free from distractions.

Choose a time when you are neither too tired nor overly energetic. For example, if you wake up feeling refreshed and then drink coffee, your nervous system may become overstimulated, which can affect the muscles it controls. This can make it difficult for your body to generate accurate "No" responses, causing you to receive "Yes" answers regardless of the question.

13.2 Key Elements of Self-Muscle Testing Explained

What is an Indicator Muscle/Body Part?

Answer: An indicator muscle or body part is the one tested for strength in response to a question. It provides the answer by either remaining strong or momentarily weakening. **For most people,** the indicator hand is the non-dominant hand.

Question: What is a Testing Hand?

Answer: The testing hand performs the muscle test by applying moderate force, usually in a vertical or horizontal direction, to the indicator muscle or body part. For most people, the testing hand is the dominant hand.

In the picture below, I demonstrate the Whole-arm Test, which primarily tests the anterior deltoid muscle. My left arm functions as the indicator arm, while my right hand (about to apply moderate downward pressure) is my testing hand.

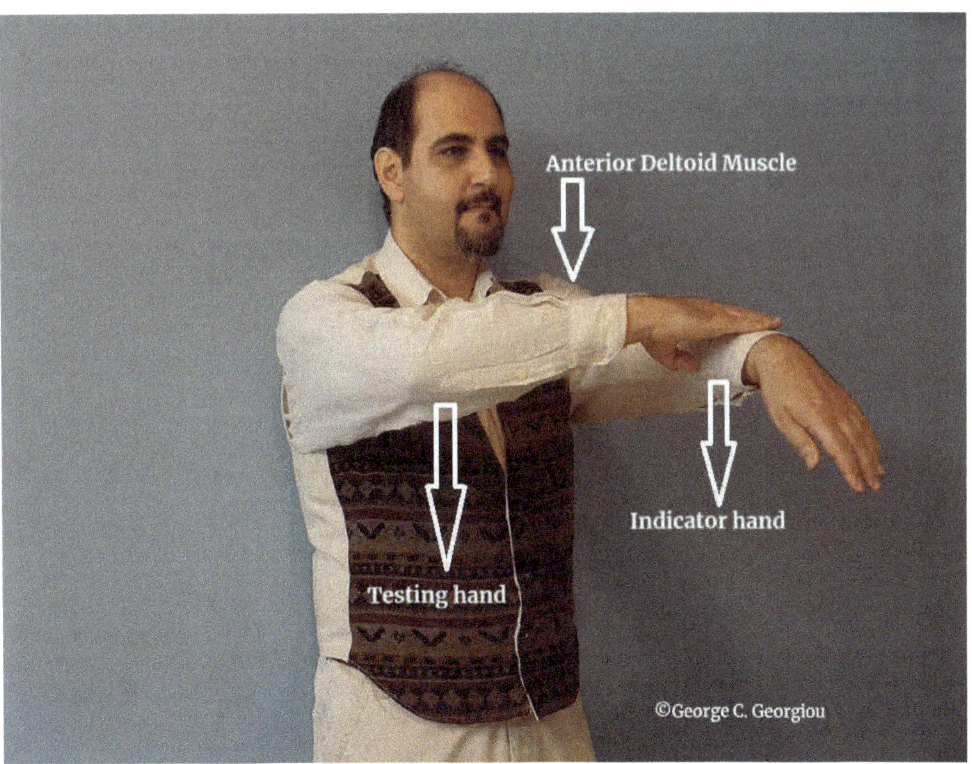

While this test is useful for demonstrations and practice, most self-muscle testing techniques involve using your fingers rather than your arm or elbow. Mastering at least two of these techniques is ideal because they are discreet and practical. You can even perform them under the table while having dinner, in case a question arises and you need a quick answer from your subconscious.

Of course, you could use the Whole-Arm Test, if you do not mind attracting attention and making people wonder whether you have escaped from a mental institution!

Question: What do the terms Strong (Locked) and Weak (Unlocked) responses mean?

Answer: After performing a self-muscle test, you will observe one of two possible responses:

- Strong or Locked Muscle – The indicator muscle remains strong when force is applied by the testing hand. This signifies a "Yes" or "True" response.

- Weak or Unlocked Muscle – The indicator muscle momentarily loses its strength and weakens when force is applied by the testing hand. This signifies a "No" or "False" response.

Here are some more examples:

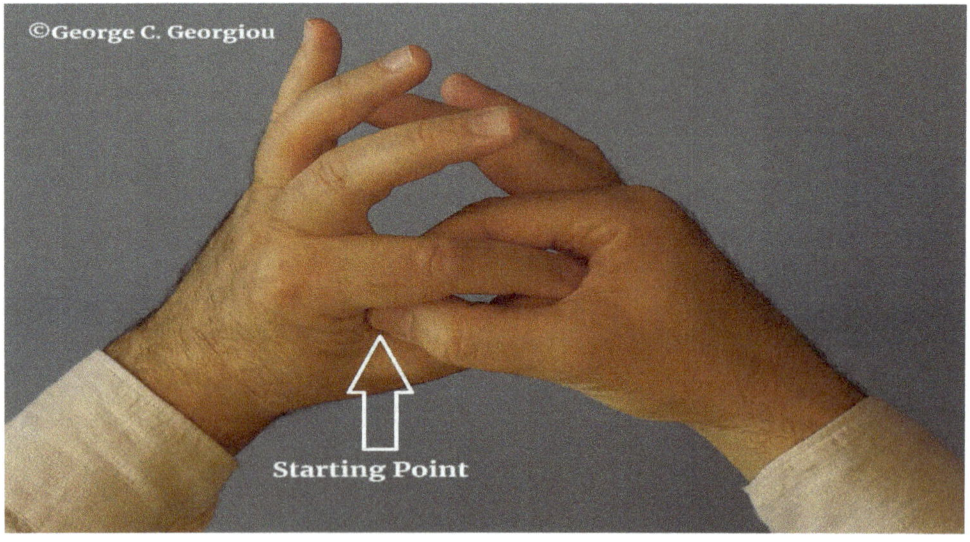

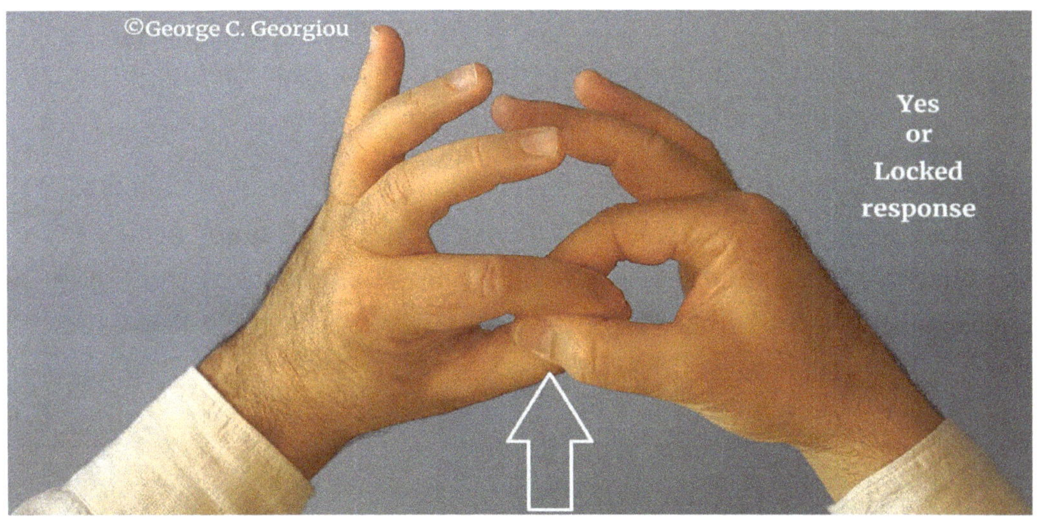

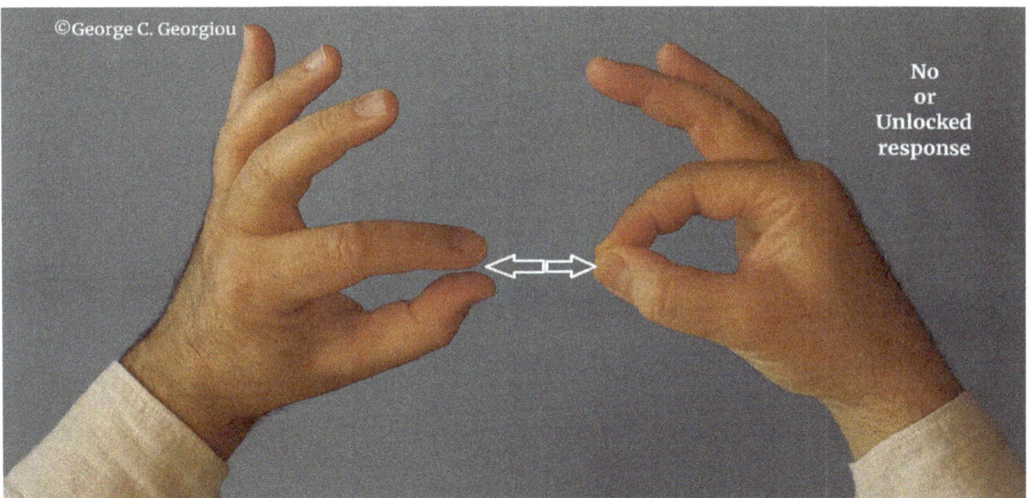

Question: What are Calibration Questions?

Answer: Calibration questions are simple, **closed-ended (yes/no)** questions with answers you already know. Examples include:

- **Is my name _________?**
- **Is today _________?**
- **Is the color of my jumper _________?**
- **Is my birth date _________?**
- **Is this the year 20_?**
- **Is my mother's name _________?**

Their purpose is to verify the accuracy of your self-muscle testing responses while also serving as a tuning tool to ensure that the muscles involved in your chosen self-muscle test are responding correctly.

However, when you want to perform self-muscle testing, you may notice that your initial responses are reversed. This is normal and usually occurs because your muscles have not yet been stimulated for this purpose or, if you prefer, they are sleeping and they give off wrong answers. After a few calibration questions, they typically adjust.

Let's assume you have prepared your questions and are ready to use your preferred self-muscle testing technique, such as the Double-Loop Self-Muscle Test (see page 92), to obtain the answers you seek. You should never jump straight into asking your questions. Even if you have adequately prepared and successfully connected with your chosen Higher Source of Knowledge and Wisdom, you ALWAYS START BY ASKING CALIBRATION QUESTIONS!

In fact, you can proceed with your session questions only after receiving three consecutive correct responses to your calibration questions.

How to Calibrate Your Self-Muscle Test Tool

Personally, I begin with using these two simple commands:

1. **"Give me a Yes"** (then test)
2. **"Give me a No"** (then test)

Or, if you prefer:

1. **"Show me a Yes"** (then test)
2. **"Show me a No"** (then test)

Repeat this process until you consistently receive three consecutive correct responses. Then, follow up with two additional calibration questions from the provided example list, or create your own based on your surroundings.

For example:

- Is the wall I am looking at pink?
- Is the color of my shoes black?

Following this process ensures that your self-muscle testing tool is calibrated correctly and provides accurate responses.

13.3 Preparing for Self-Muscle Testing: What You Need to Know

Before introducing the eight ways to perform self-muscle testing, I want to share some important insights and refresh key concepts. These will help you align with the process and improve your results.

The first key point is understanding what we are trying to achieve. We aim to establish communication with a Higher Source of Knowledge and Wisdom and receive guidance. Since we are not psychics, at least not yet, we rely on self-muscle testing as a divination tool to obtain answers. By asking the right questions and presenting different options, we allow our source to indicate the best one.

"The kind of reality we live in is shaped by the level of questions beyond the ordinary we dare to ask and explore."

- George C. Georgiou

Next, it is essential to recognize how self-muscle testing works. After asking a question, the body momentarily adjusts the strength of a specific muscle, making it either strong or weak. This shift translates into a *yes* or *no* response.

Another crucial point to remember is that if we do not consciously choose to connect with a specific Higher Source of Knowledge and Wisdom, the answers we receive will default to our subconscious mind, as it naturally serves as our primary higher source of knowledge and wisdom.

For most people, the indicator arm is the non-dominant hand, while the testing arm is the dominant one. However, if you feel more comfortable with the opposite arrangement, that's perfectly fine.

All self-muscle tests can be performed while standing or sitting. If you are sitting, ensure your upper body is straight.

I have chosen the **whole-arm self-muscle test** as the first technique to demonstrate, as it is one of the easiest ways to illustrate these principles in action.

13.4 Finding Your Ideal Self-Muscle Testing Method

Statistically speaking, over the years of teaching these techniques, I have observed that even though I demonstrate eight different self-muscle testing methods, about 80 percent of participants trust and feel comfortable using only one or two of them. Only about 10 percent feel equally confident using a third method as well.

This is why we are fortunate to have so many self-muscle testing methods, including various combinations, available to us. If there were only one or two options, many people would struggle to resonate with any of them.

Not every technique suits everyone. You need to experiment with all of them and determine which two feel the most natural and comfortable, and most importantly, provide the most accurate responses!

To help you identify your ideal techniques, I have developed a simple two-point grading system based on **Comfortability** and **Accuracy**:

- **Comfortability** – This refers to how naturally the technique comes to you and how comfortable it feels when performing it. The highest possible score for this criterion is **10 out of 10 (10/10)**.
- **Accuracy** – This measures how precise the responses are. For each technique and finger combination, we will ask five questions. Each correct answer is worth two points, making the highest possible accuracy score **10/10**.

By using this system, you can confidently determine which self-muscle testing methods work best for you.

Here is an example:

Name of the technique	Comfortability	Accuracy
Single-loop test	6/10	8/10

Please decide where you will record your answers. Will it be in this book, on a separate sheet of paper, or in a file on your computer?

13.5 How to Perform the Following Self-Muscle Testing Techniques for Divination:

1. Whole-arm test technique
Muscle Tested: Anterior Deltoid

Step 1: Position Yourself: The indicator arm should be fully extended at shoulder level, forming a 90° angle. The elbow should also be fully extended, with the hand and fingers relaxed, and pointing downward. The testing hand is placed just before the wrist joint of the indicator arm. This is your initial position that you need to assume before performing the test.

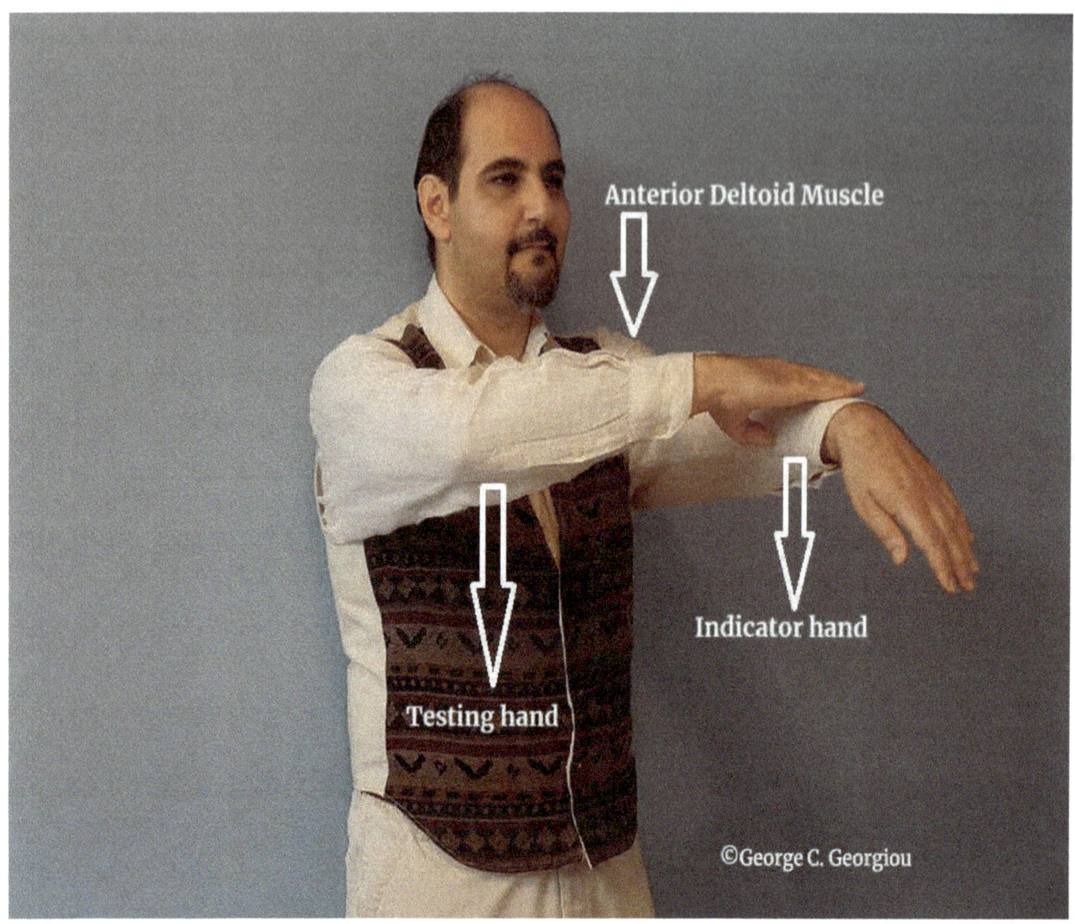

Step 2: Establishing Force and Resistance

Focus on your indicator arm at the point where the testing hand is placed. Using your testing hand, apply a downward force on the indicator arm with about 50 percent of your total strength while simultaneously engaging your indicator arm to maintain its horizontal position. In other words, the indicator arm resists the downward pressure applied by the testing hand. If done correctly, both arms should remain stable in their original position.

Before proceeding, practice this sequence a few times, starting from steps 1 and 2. Relax your arms, then assume the correct position and use your testing hand to apply a downward force of about 50 percent of your total strength, while your indicator arm resists with equal force.

Step 3: Perform a Calibration Test

Focus on your indicator arm, ensuring it remains horizontal, strong, and firm. Now, ask the following calibration question:

"My name is ..." (Say your real name.)

After a two-second pause, push down with your testing hand, this time using 70 percent of your total strength. Your indicator arm should remain firm and strong or move only slightly downward.

If your arm moved noticeably downward, which it should not, repeat this exact step until you get three consecutive lock responses or yes responses.

What happens here is that your subconscious automatically increases the strength of the indicator arm to resist the increased pressure, thus giving you a Yes response. The same but opposite mechanism applies for a No answer. The subconscious automatically decreases the strength of the indicator arm, and when it weakens, the indicator arm or finger unlocks, showing you a No response.

Next, ask: **"My name is ..."** (Say a fake name, preferably of the opposite sex.) After a two-second pause, push down with your testing hand using no more than 70% of your total strength. This time, your arm should weaken and drop, indicating a "no" or false answer.

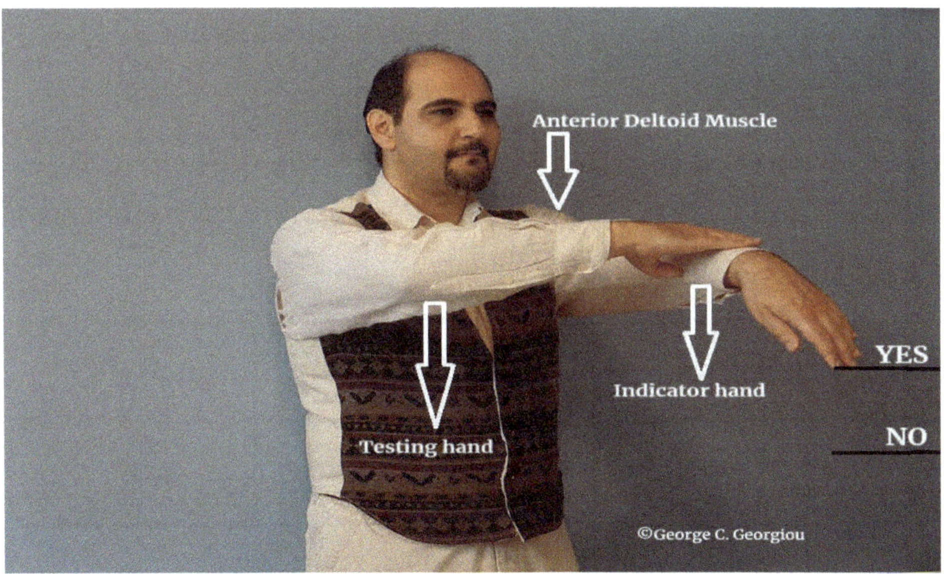

Step 4: Take a 15-Minute Break

At this point, take a **15-minute** break to allow your arm muscles to relax. Do not exceed this time, as you are in the correct mental state, and we want to keep you there. Skipping this break will result in false answers due to fatigued muscles, leading to frustration and disappointment!

Step 5: Evaluate the Technique

After your break, repeat Steps 1 to 3. This time around, we need to evaluate how natural the technique feels to you, or how comfortable you are performing it, and how accurate it is in providing answers. To do this, you will ask yourself five questions and perform the self-muscle test for each. Each correct answer is worth two points.

Once finished, record your score. Here are some calibration questions to ask yourself:

1. Is today _________? (Say the wrong day and test.)
2. Is the color of my eyes _________? (Say the correct color and test.)
3. Is my birth date _________? (Say the wrong birth date and test.)
4. Is this the year 20_? (Say the correct year and test.)
5. Is my mother's name _________? (Say the wrong name and test.)

Just to ensure clarity, if your arm remained strong for the two correct answers and weakened for the three false answers, you answered everything correctly, earning a perfect score of 10/10.

Name of the technique	Comfortability	Accuracy
Whole-arm Test	/10	/10

Remember, consistent practice leads to mastery. Follow the instructions carefully, and you will become a skilled and confident self-muscle tester for divination.

A Few Key Notes Before Moving Forward

If you have followed my instructions carefully up to this point, you should now have a good idea about self-muscle testing and what it feels like to receive yes or no answers. Now, I will guide you through seven additional self-muscle testing techniques and point out their many variations, which you must also try out.

Exploring these different methods is essential because it allows you to discover which ones feel the most natural and comfortable and, most importantly, deliver accurate answers. Once you identify the two techniques that work best for you, the rest will become unnecessary. You will rely only on those two for the rest of your life. Using the same techniques strengthens your connection to your chosen Higher Source of Knowledge and Wisdom, ensuring faster, smoother, and more reliable answers.

As you experiment with the various techniques and their variations, you will notice that I did not include those that involve the little finger (also known as the pinky finger). Anatomically and physiologically, it is a weaker finger and is more prone to producing false negative responses. This means that even when your chosen source intends to provide you with a yes answer, the pinky finger will instead give you a no answer.

The only exception to this rule is the self-muscle testing technique number five, which involves the Opponens Pollicis Longus muscle. This technique functions differently, and I will explain it in detail when we reach that section.

2) **Single-loop Test Technique.**
Muscle Tested: Flexor digitorum muscles

Use your thumb and index finger of your indicator hand to form a loop. Apply approximately 30% of your total finger strength, gently maintaining the integrity of the indicator loop.

To perform the test, place the index finger of your testing hand at the web area at the base of the thumb on your indicator hand. This is your starting position.

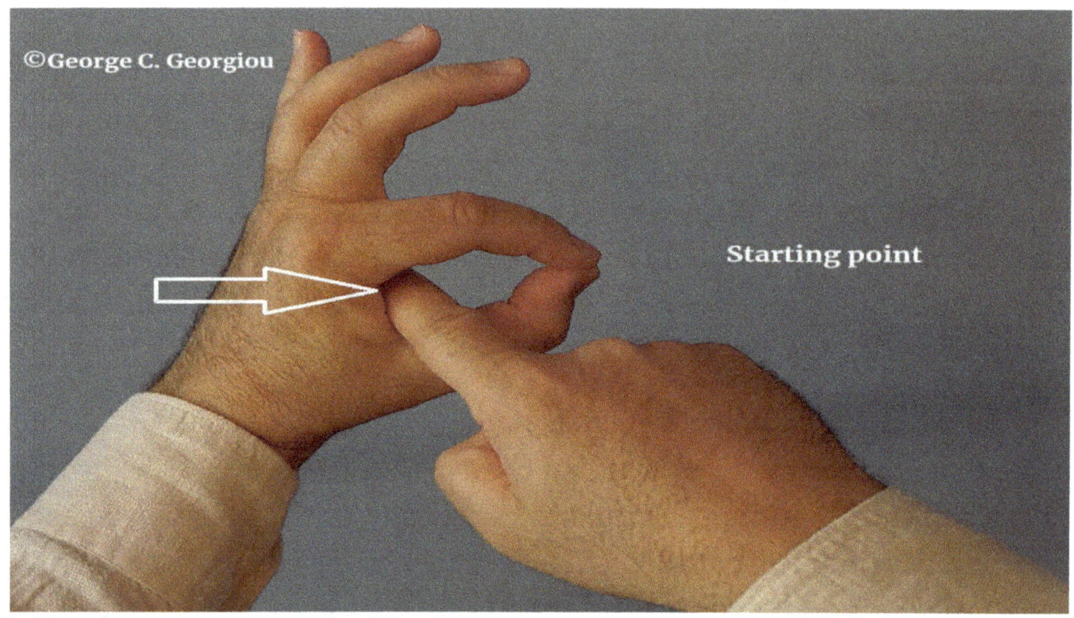

Then, ask your question, pause for two seconds, and swiftly move your testing finger toward the point where the two fingers of the indicator hand meet, as if attempting to break the loop.

A "yes" answer occurs when the testing finger stops where the two fingers of the indicator hand meet. A "no" answer occurs when the testing finger breaks the loop.

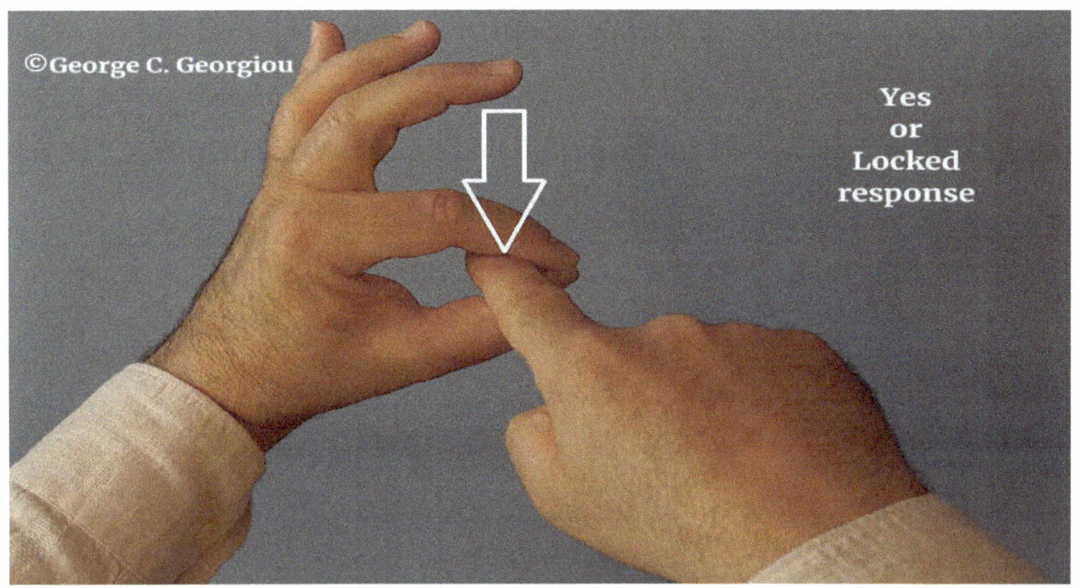

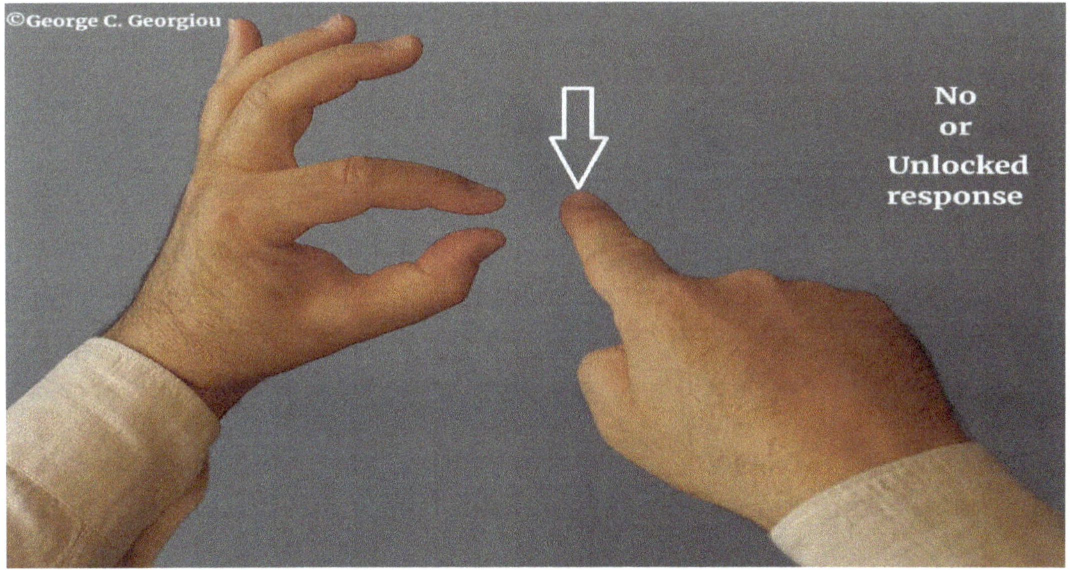

Before asking the five calibration questions on page 80, begin by testing the following:

1. **"Give me a Yes"** (then test)
2. **"Give me a No"** (then test)

Repeat until you have a clear sense of the strong response "Yes" and the weak response for "No."

Practice this technique and its variations, recording your outcomes. Use the calibration questions on page 80 to ensure accuracy.

Variation 1: Loop made with thumb and index finger.
Comfortability: **/10** Accuracy: **/10**

Variation 2: Loop made with thumb and middle finger.
Comfortability: **/10** Accuracy: **/10**

Variation 3: Loop made with thumb and ring finger.
Comfortability: **/10** Accuracy: **/10**

3) Double-loop test technique.

Muscle Tested: Flexor digitorum muscles

Use your thumb and index finger of your indicator hand to form a loop. Use your thumb and index finger of your testing hand to form a loop. Next, interlock them like two rings in a chain. Apply approximately 30% of your total finger strength to all the fingers involved in forming the rings, gently maintaining the integrity of both rings.

Begin by placing the two joined fingers of your testing hand at the web area at the base of the thumb on your indicator hand. This is your starting position.

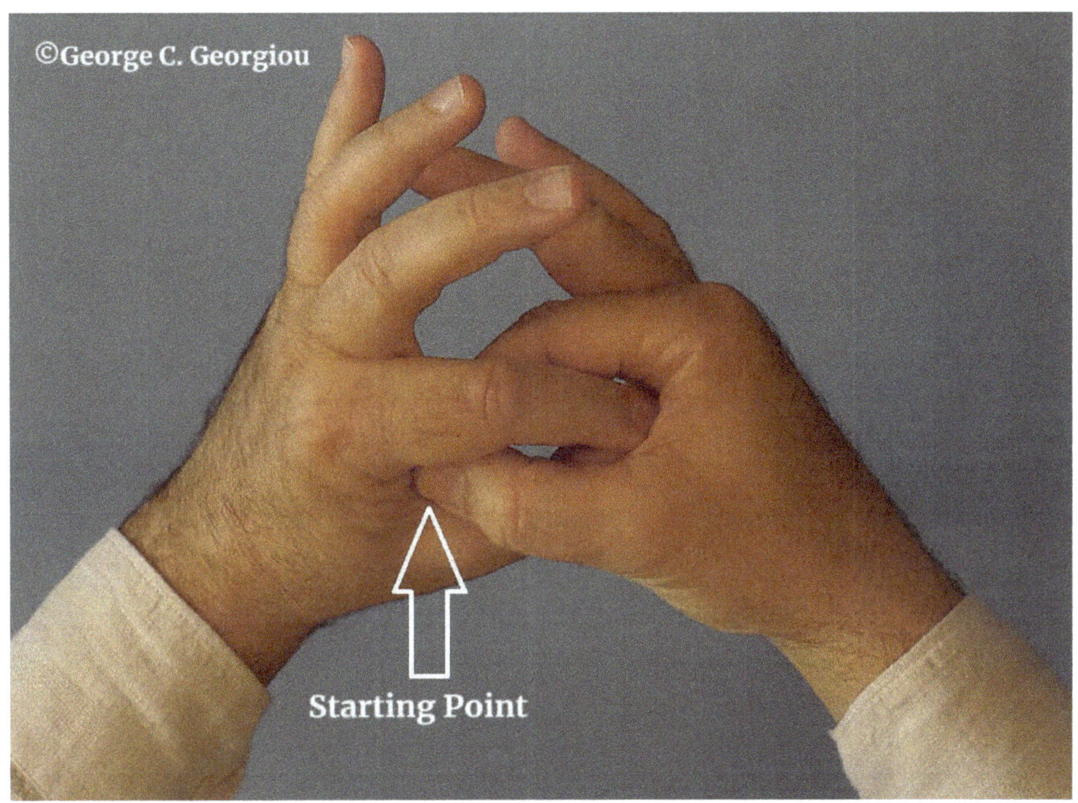

A "yes" answer occurs when the testing finger stops where the two fingers of the indicator hand meet (remains locked). A "no" answer occurs when the testing finger breaks the loop (unlock).

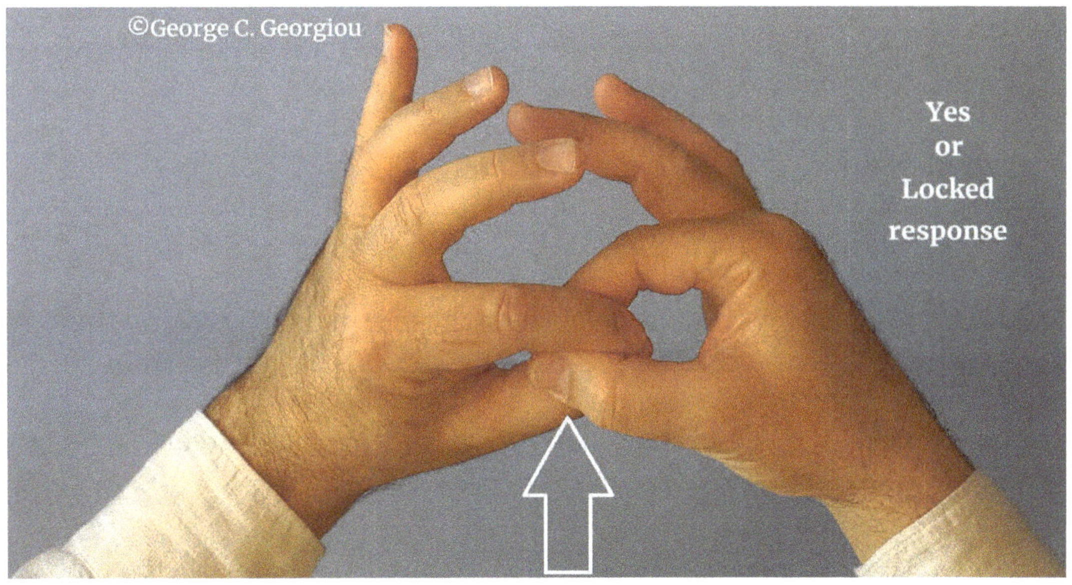

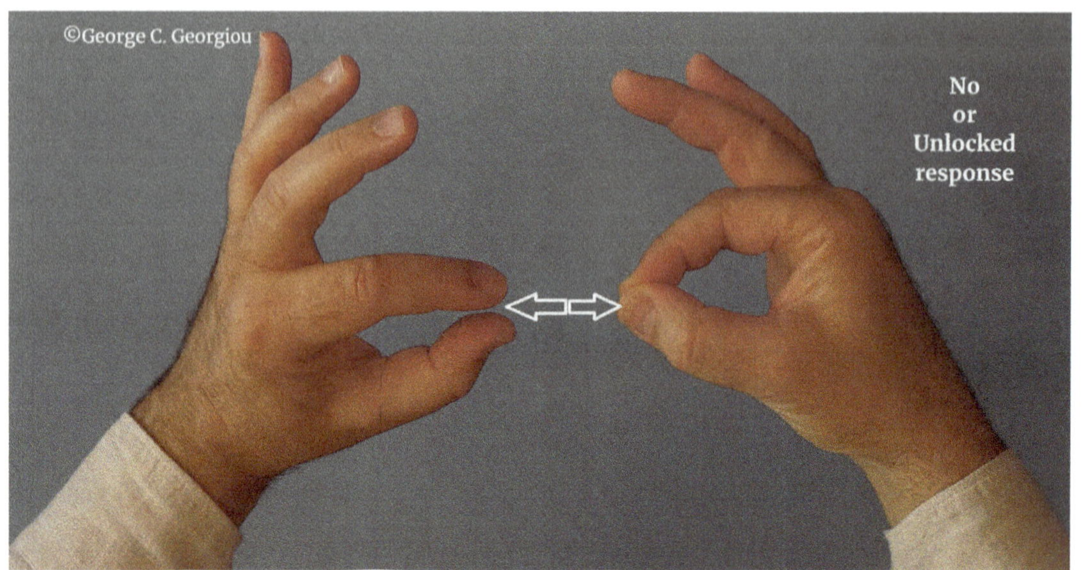

To perform the test, ask your question, pause for two seconds, and gently pull your testing hand away from the indicator hand at the point where the two fingers meet.

This technique, along with the one that follows, offers the most variations, a total of nine. You need to try all of them and grade each one. While this may seem daunting, remember that you only need to do it once. About 35% of my seminar participants have found their ideal and permanent self-muscle test within one of the finger combinations listed below.

Before asking the five calibration questions on page 80, begin by testing the following:

1. **"Give me a Yes"** (then test)
2. **"Give me a No"** (then test)

Repeat until you have a clear sense of the strong response "Yes" and the weak response for "No."

Practice this technique and its variations, recording your outcomes. Use the calibration questions on page 80 to ensure accuracy.

Variations:

1) Testing hand: thumb and index finger – Indicator hand: thumb and index finger
Comfortability: **/10** Accuracy: **/10**

2) Testing hand: thumb and index finger – Indicator hand: thumb and middle finger
Comfortability: **/10** Accuracy: **/10**

3) Testing hand: thumb and index finger – Indicator hand: thumb and ring finger
Comfortability: **/10** Accuracy: **/10**

4) Testing hand: thumb and middle finger – Indicator hand: thumb and index finger
Comfortability: **/10** Accuracy: **/10**

5) Testing hand: thumb and middle finger – Indicator hand: thumb and middle finger
Comfortability: **/10** Accuracy: **/10**

6) Testing hand: thumb and middle finger – Indicator hand: thumb and ring finger
Comfortability: **/10** Accuracy: **/10**

7) Testing hand: thumb and ring finger – Indicator hand: thumb and index finger
Comfortability: **/10** Accuracy: **/10**

8) Testing hand: thumb and ring finger – Indicator hand: thumb and middle finger
Comfortability: **/10** Accuracy: **/10**

9) Testing hand: thumb and ring finger – Indicator hand: thumb and ring finger
Comfortability: **/10** Accuracy: **/10**

4) Finger-wedge test technique.

Muscle Tested: Flexor digitorum muscles

There are two approaches to this technique, and you can use whichever one feels better for you. For the first approach, I will simply show what it looks like, and then I will use the second one for the instructions, as the responses appear clearer with that approach.

Step 1: Use your thumb and index finger of your indicator hand to form a loop. Use your thumb and index finger of your testing hand to form a loop.

Step 2: The loop of the testing hand is then squeezed inside the loop of the indicator hand, forming a wedge shape. This can be done either from the front, like this:

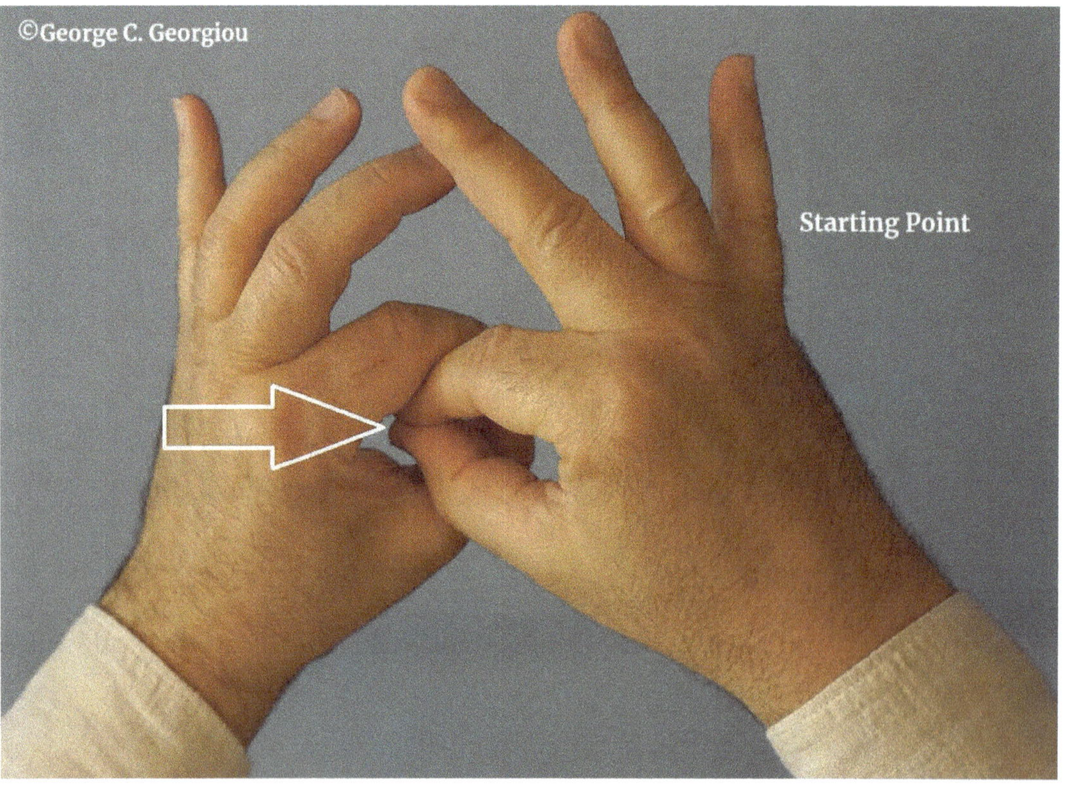

or from the back, like this:

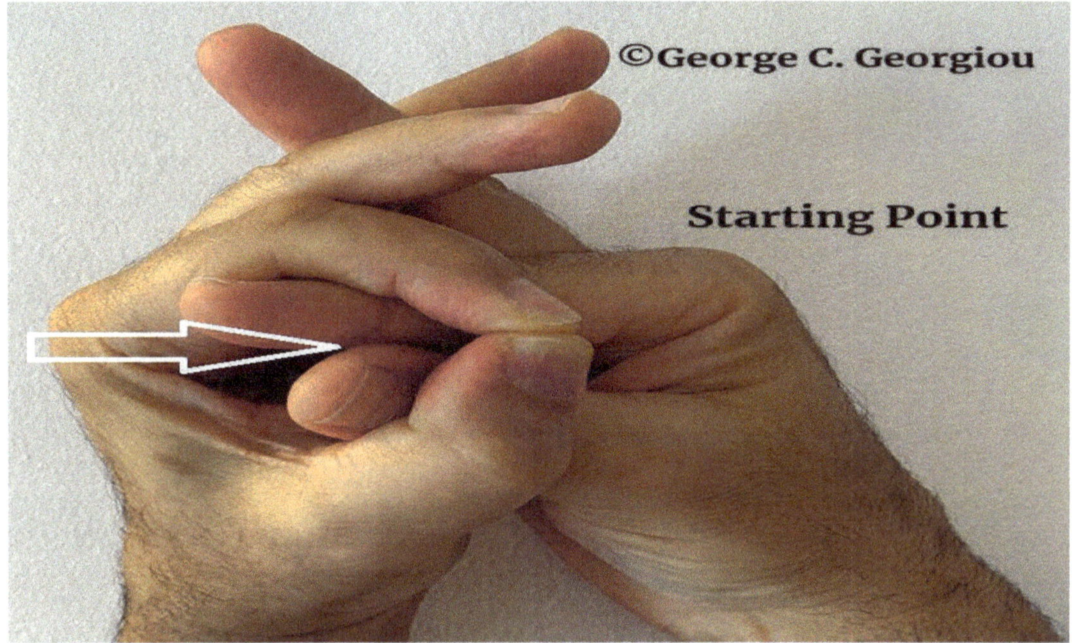

These two pictures also illustrate the starting point for each approach.

Step 3: Apply approximately 30% of your total finger strength, gently maintaining the integrity of the indicator loop.

To perform the test, ask your question, pause for two seconds, and then apply a small burst of strength to separate the wedge fingers of your testing hand, as if trying to force them apart.

A "yes" answer occurs when the fingers of the indicator hand remain locked, maintaining the loop. A "no" answer occurs when the fingers unlock, meaning the loop breaks apart.

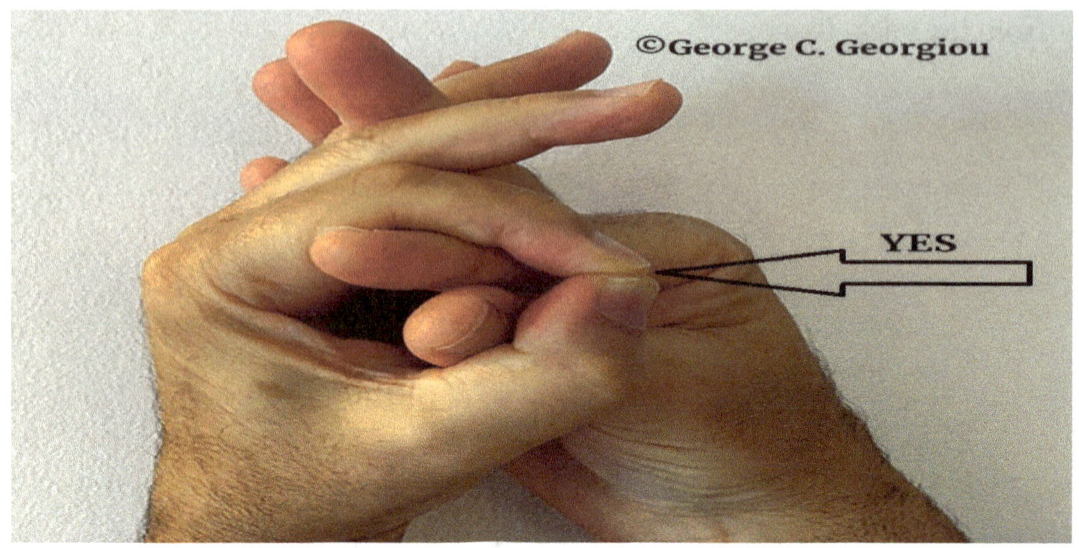

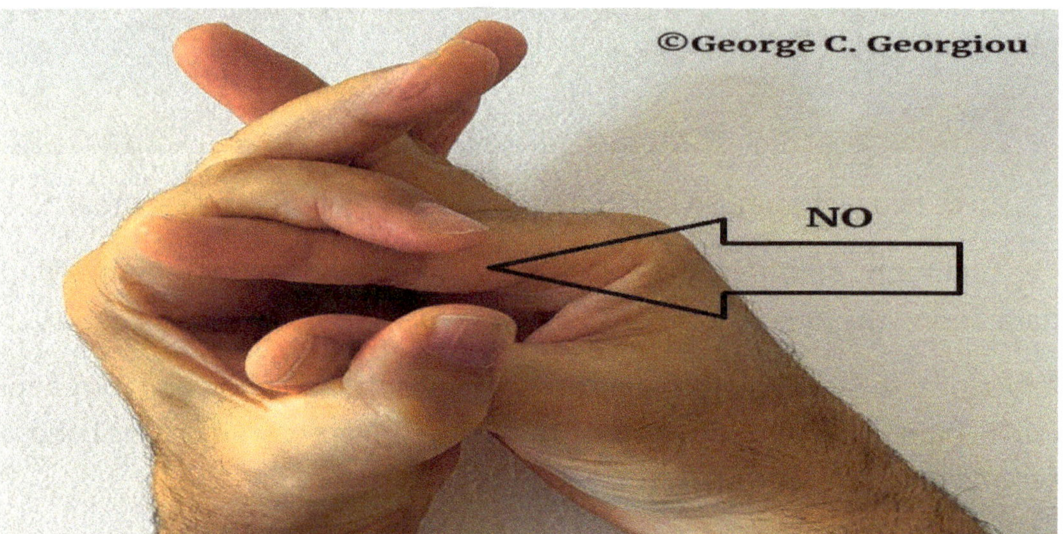

By now, I'm sure you've noticed that in many cases, the starting point and a Yes response are the same.

Like the previous technique, this method offers nine variations. You need to test and grade each one, as 35% of my seminar participants have found their ideal and permanent self-muscle test within one of the finger combinations listed below.

Before asking the five calibration questions on page 80, begin by testing the following:

1. **"Give me a Yes"** (then test)
2. **"Give me a No"** (then test)

Repeat until you have a clear sense of the strong response "Yes" and the weak response for "No."

Practice this technique and its variations, recording your outcomes. Use the calibration questions on page 80 to ensure accuracy.

Variations:

1) Testing hand: thumb and index finger – Indicator hand: thumb and index finger
Comfortability: **/10** Accuracy: **/10**

2) Testing hand: thumb and index finger – Indicator hand: thumb and middle finger
Comfortability: **/10** Accuracy: **/10**

3) Testing hand: thumb and index finger – Indicator hand: thumb and ring finger
Comfortability: **/10** Accuracy: **/10**

4) Testing hand: thumb and middle finger – Indicator hand: thumb and index finger
Comfortability: **/10** Accuracy: **/10**

5) Testing hand: thumb and middle finger – Indicator hand: thumb and middle finger
Comfortability: **/10** Accuracy: **/10**

6) Testing hand: thumb and middle finger – Indicator hand: thumb and ring finger
Comfortability: **/10** Accuracy: **/10**

7) Testing hand: thumb and ring finger – Indicator hand: thumb and index finger
Comfortability: **/10** Accuracy: **/10**

8) Testing hand: thumb and ring finger – Indicator hand: thumb and middle finger

Comfortability: **/10** Accuracy: **/10**

9) Testing hand: thumb and ring finger – Indicator hand: thumb and ring finger

Comfortability: **/10** Accuracy: **/10**

5) Thumb-pinky loop test technique

Muscle Tested: Opponens Pollicis Longus

Use your thumb and little finger (pinky finger) of your indicator hand to form a loop. Use your thumb and index finger of your testing hand to form a wedge. Next, insert the wedge-shaped fingers of your testing hand inside the loop created by your indicator hand. This is your starting position.

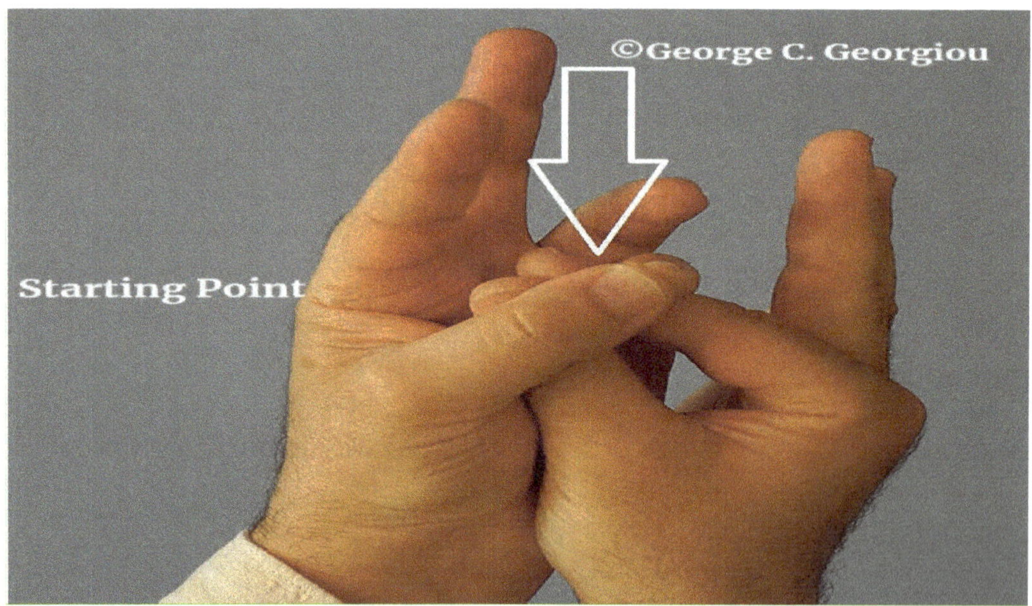

Apply approximately 30% of your total finger strength, gently maintaining the integrity of the indicator loop.

To perform the test, ask your question, pause for two seconds, and then apply a small burst of strength to separate the wedge fingers of your testing hand, as if trying to force them apart.

A "yes" answer occurs when the fingers of the indicator hand remain locked, keeping the loop intact. A "no" answer occurs when the fingers unlock, breaking the loop.

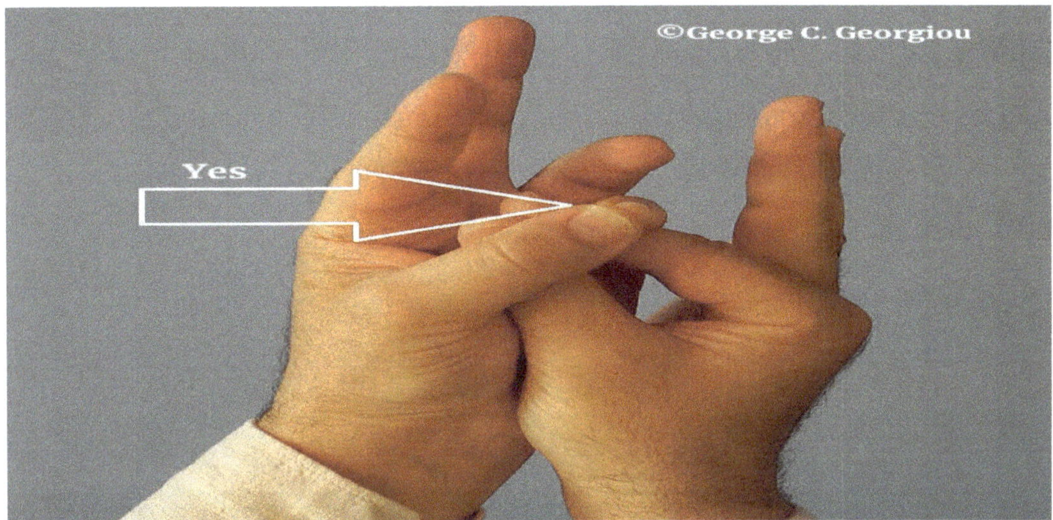

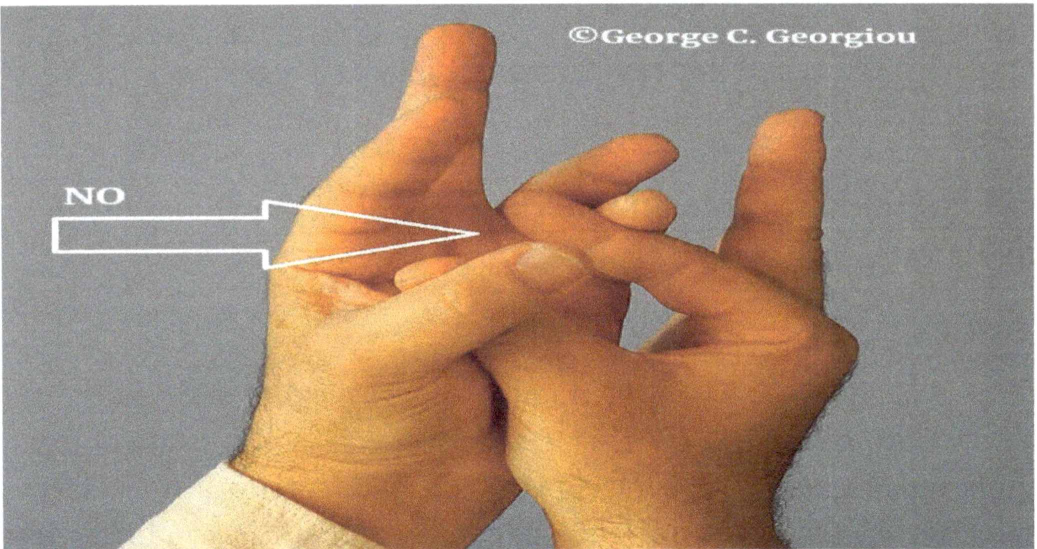

This method has three variations and is considered highly accurate compared to other tests involving the little finger. For this reason, I chose not to include those variations in the other techniques.

Before asking the five calibration questions on page 80, begin by testing the following:

1. **"Give me a Yes"** (then test)
2. **"Give me a No"** (then test)

Repeat until you have a clear sense of the strong response "Yes" and the weak response for "No."

Practice this technique and its variations, recording your outcomes. Use the calibration questions on page 80 to ensure accuracy.

Variations:

(The indicator hand and finger remain the same in all variations.)

1) Testing hand: thumb and index finger forming the wedge
Comfortability: /10 Accuracy: /10

2) Testing hand: thumb and middle finger forming the wedge
Comfortability: /10 Accuracy: /10

3) Testing hand: thumb and ring finger forming the wedge
Comfortability: /10 Accuracy: /10

6. Flexed-elbow test technique.

Muscle Tested: Brachioradialis

Side Note:

This is a modified version of the traditional physiological muscle test. Based on years of experience, I've made a few simple adjustments that have significantly increased both its accuracy and comfort. It's especially appreciated by those who, for various reasons, cannot perform finger-based techniques.

To perform this technique, begin by flexing your indicator forearm at a 120° angle and resting it on a hard surface, such as a desk or a table. The forearm should stay firm but not overly tense. The hand and fingers should be completely relaxed and pointing downward. Position your testing hand on the top side of the indicator hand, over the wrist. This is your starting position.

To perform the test, ask your question, then apply vertical downward pressure using the testing hand at the contact point, using about **40%** of your total strength.

A **"yes"** response occurs when the indicator forearm remains locked or shows only a slight downward movement. A **"no"** response occurs when the forearm weakens and drops noticeably. A common sign of a "no" answer is when the fingers of the indicator hand touch the table or surface below.

Before proceeding with the five calibration questions on page 80, start with the following:

1. "Give me a Yes" (then test)

2. "Give me a No" (then test)

Repeat until you have a clear sense of the strong response "Yes" and the weak response for "No."

Practice this technique and record your outcomes. Use the calibration questions on page 80 to ensure accuracy.

7) Scissor-fingers test technique

Muscle Tested: Extensor and abductor digitorum muscles

A general remark about the Scissor Fingers Test Technique, as well as the following Finger on Finger Test Technique, is that both tend to be much less effective for most people. Many find them uncomfortable to perform and struggle to achieve consistently accurate results. This is not accidental, as we are using two finger muscles that are naturally small and weak. For these reasons, I have never used them myself. That said, in the spirit of making this book as thorough and inclusive as possible, I have decided to include them. To be fair, a small number of my workshop participants, fewer than five percent, have reported success with these two methods. In fact, they found them comfortable and were able to receive clear and reliable answers, so it feels only right to share them with you as well.

Your indicator hand forms the "scissors" by fully extending the index and middle fingers straight out and apart. The remaining fingers, the thumb, ring, and pinky, are curled out of the way, as shown in the picture below.

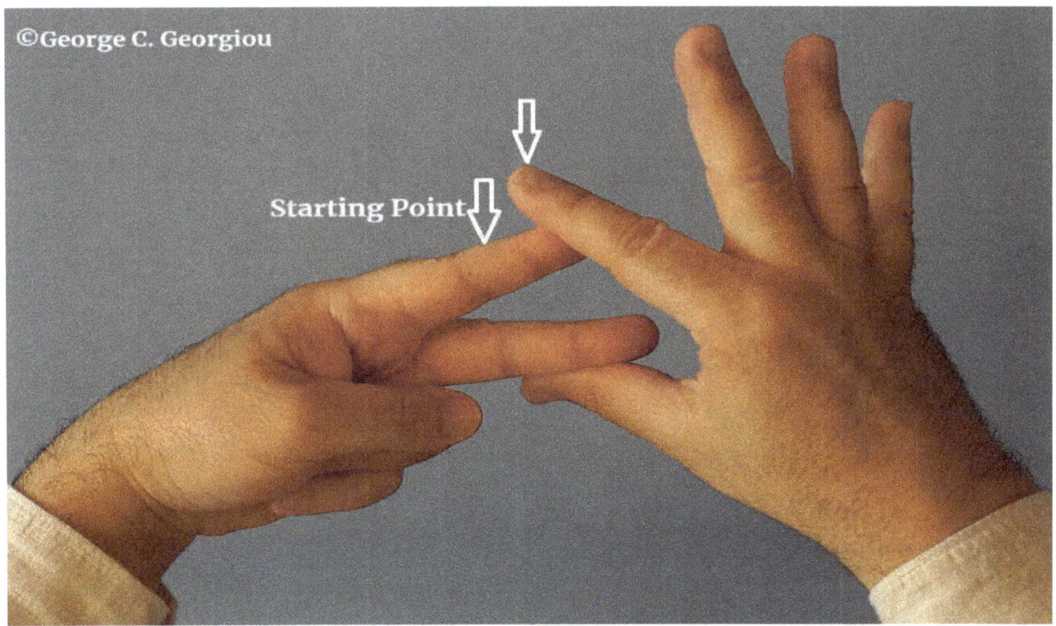

To perform the test, use the thumb and index finger of your testing hand. Place the index finger above the index indicator finger, either towards the edge of the finger or positioned midway between the two finger creases (distal and middle). The thumb of the testing hand should be placed beneath the middle indicator finger, also midway between the two creases. This is your starting position.

Before initiating the muscle test, focus your attention on the extended fingers of your indicator hand. Make them firm and strong by engaging your full finger strength. Then, ask your question, pause for two seconds, and gently but firmly pinch the sides of the indicator fingers.

A "yes" response occurs when the indicator fingers remain firm or move slightly closer together, stopping around the white line shown in the picture. A "no" response occurs when they move significantly closer or come into contact with each other.

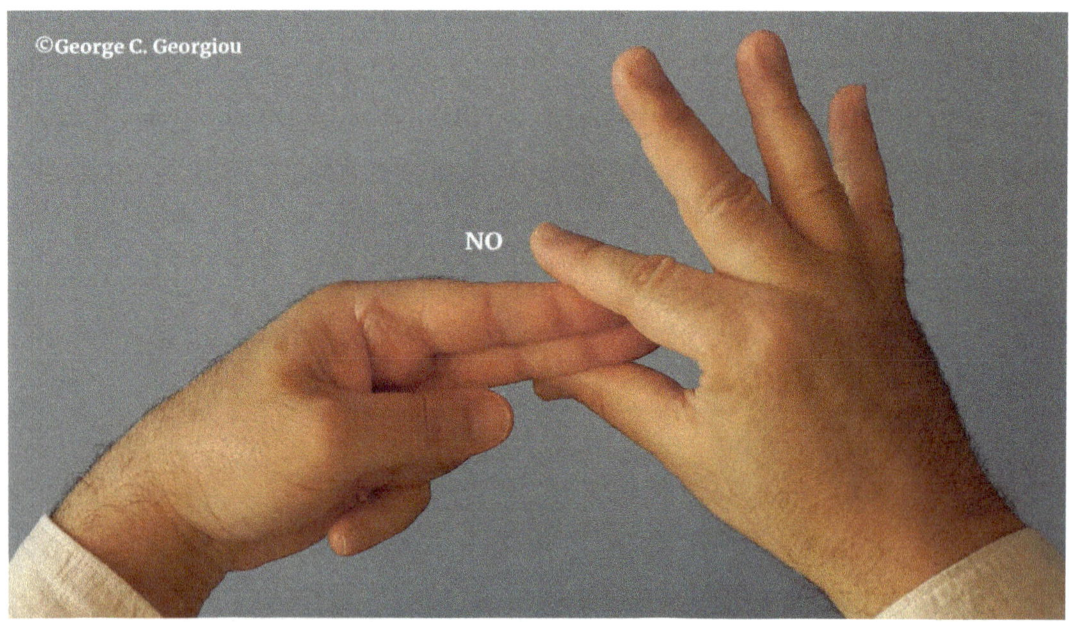

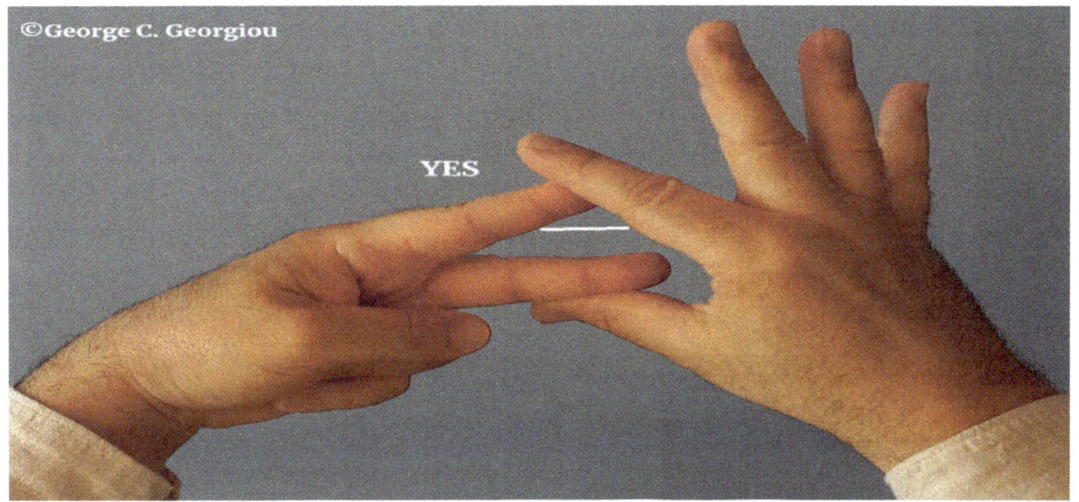

Before proceeding with the five calibration questions on page 80, start with the following:

1. "Give me a Yes" (then test)
2. "Give me a No" (then test)

Repeat until you have a clear sense of the strong response "Yes" and the weak response for "No."

Practice this technique and record your outcomes. Use the calibration questions on page 80 to ensure accuracy.

Please note that there are no other finger variations for this technique.

8. The finger-on-finger test technique

Muscle Tested: Extensor digitorum muscles

Very few people can perform this test successfully, and I am certainly not one of them. It is both anatomically and biomechanically challenging, making it difficult to distinguish between the two possible answers. However, those who can manage it are considered fortunate, as this technique allows them to test something with one hand while keeping the other free to point or touch the object in question.

This one-handed technique can be performed by pressing the middle finger against the index finger or vice versa. The top finger always performs the test by pushing downward, while the lower finger resists and indicates the answer.

To set up the test, curl the top (testing) finger into a clear half-circle over the indicator finger, placing its fingertip just below the nail of the lower finger. This is your starting position.

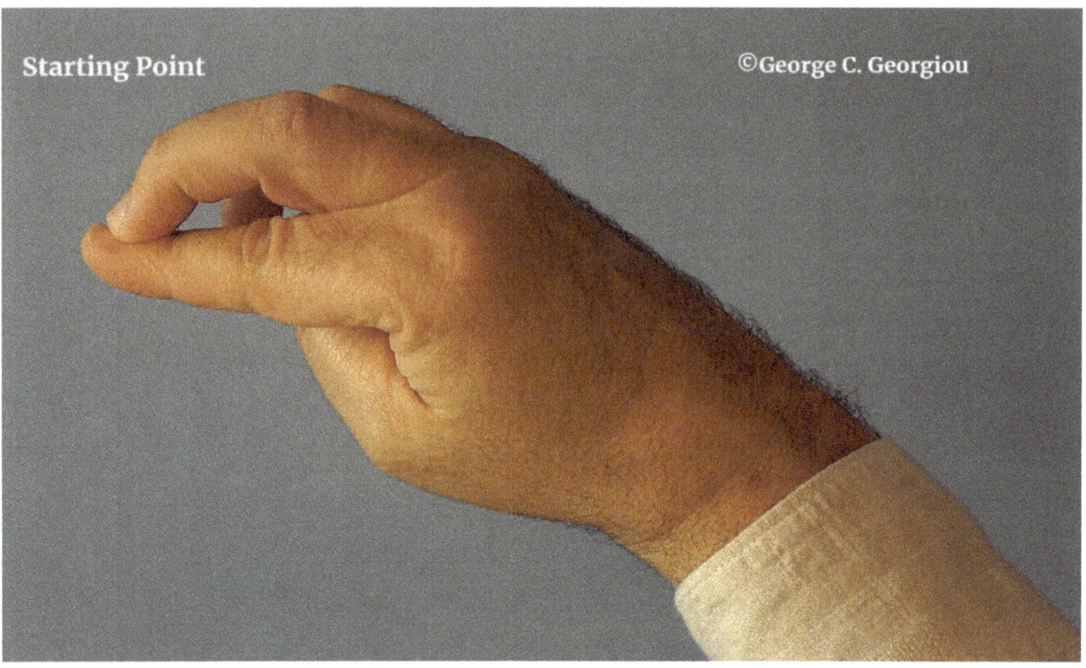

Before initiating the muscle test, focus your attention on your extended indicator finger and engage it with full strength, making it firm and steady. Then, ask your question, pause for two seconds, and have the testing finger gently but firmly press down on the indicator finger.

A "yes" response occurs when the indicator finger stays firm or moves only slightly downward. A "no" response occurs when the indicator finger completely weakens and drops to a downward angle.

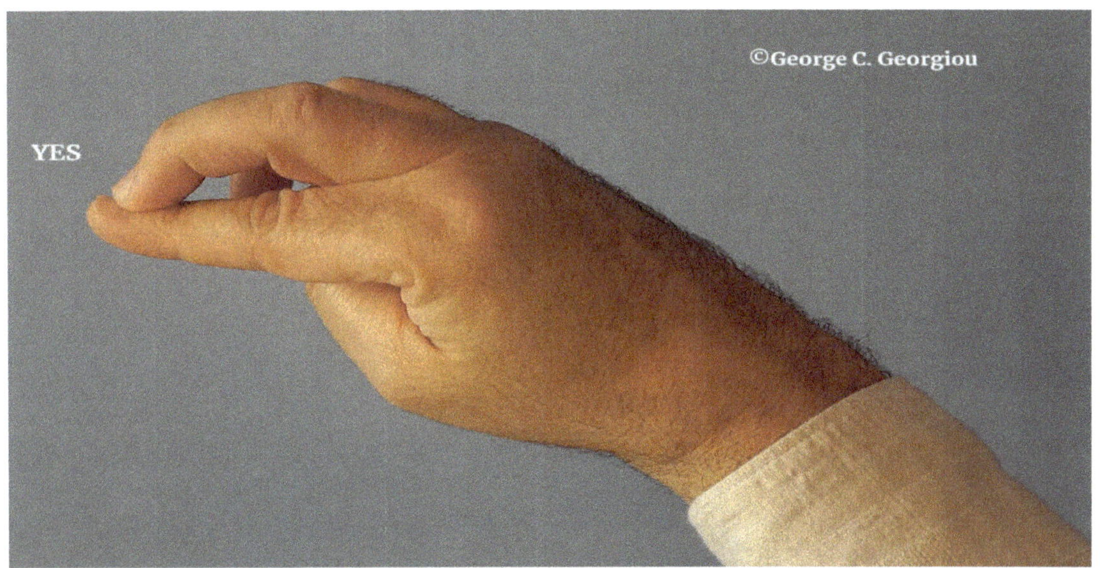

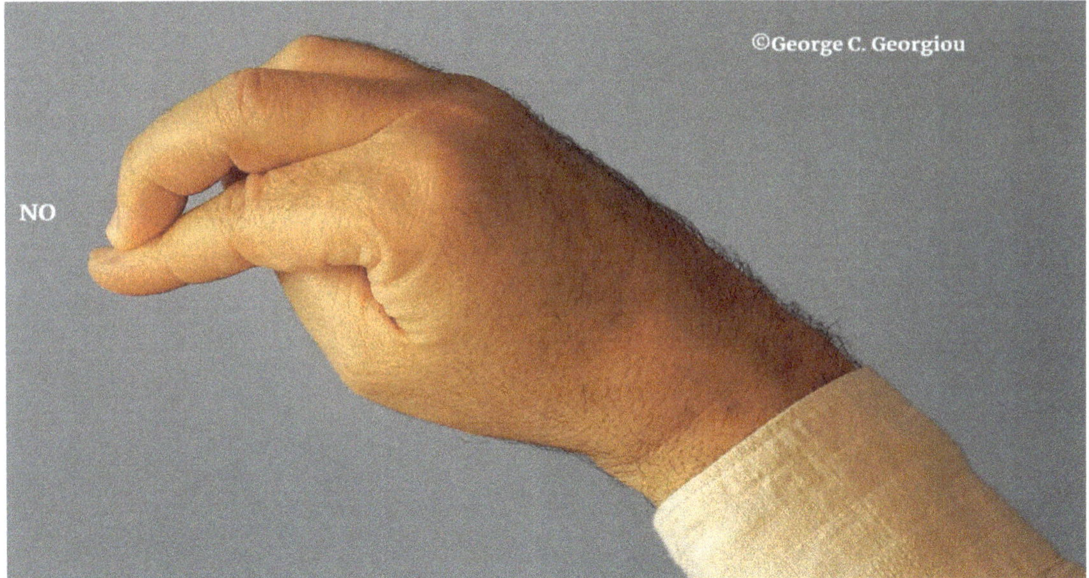

Before proceeding with the five calibration questions on page 80, start with the following:

1. "Give me a Yes" (then test)
2. "Give me a No" (then test)

Repeat until you have a clear sense of the strong response "Yes" and the weak response for "No."

Practice this technique and record your outcomes. Use the calibration questions on page 80 to ensure accuracy.

The two variations are:

1) Testing finger: Index finger
   Indicator finger: Middle finger
   Comfortability: **/10** Accuracy: **/10**

2) Testing finger: Middle finger
   Indicator finger: Index finger
   Comfortability: /10 Accuracy: /10

"The will to win, the desire to succeed, the urge to reach your full potential... these are the keys that will unlock the door to personal excellence."

— *Confucius*

CHAPTER 14

Three Approaches to Self-Muscle Testing for Divination Purposes

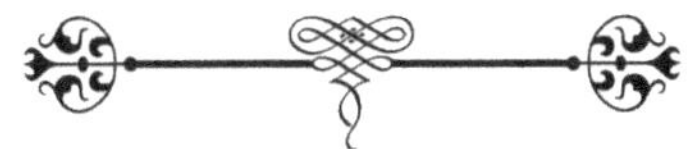

14.1 Introduction

Before you start self-muscle testing everything that moves, every thought and idea that crosses your mind, or worse, testing major life decisions, it's crucial to understand one key truth. Most Higher Sources of Knowledge and Wisdom vibrate at a much higher frequency. Without raising your vibration, these sources will remain out of reach. Even if you've followed my protocols, elevated your frequency, and gained access to your preferred Higher Source, that alone does not guarantee you'll receive an answer. Each Higher Source has its own set of rules and conditions, which I explained in detail earlier in the book.

Additionally, as you begin your journey of connecting with and consulting your Higher Sources of Knowledge and Wisdom, there are three main contra-indications to self-muscle testing for divination purposes. If you find yourself in any of the following situations, you must avoid performing self-muscle testing or relying on the answers you receive, as they will likely be wrong anywhere from 80% to 100% of the time. In these cases, you may either receive the opposite answer or your answer may be ego- or fear-based.

The first situation is when your consciousness has been negatively altered, such as after consuming drugs, alcohol, medications with psychotropic effects, coffee, nicotine, or sugar. To address this, if you've consumed drugs or alcohol, wait at least 48 hours before performing self-muscle testing, and make sure to drink plenty of water during this time.

As for medications with psychotropic effects, since you can't stop taking them or go against your doctor's advice, I recommend performing self-muscle testing close to the time you take your next dose. This ensures that the time between doses is as long as possible. Furthermore, after receiving your answer, discussing it with a friend, your psychiatrist, or psychologist is essential.

I know you may think it's your life, and you can make your own decisions, but trust me, in this situation, sharing your answer or chosen option with others can help you refine your choices and improve the outcome. Remember the saying: **two heads are better than one!**

If you've consumed coffee, nicotine, or sugar within 2 to 3 hours of your divination session, you may experience false positives due to the stimulation they cause in your central nervous system. This stimulation can make producing a "no" answer difficult because the body cannot relax the indicator muscle, therefore receiving only "yes" answers.

The second situation occurs when you have a small or medium injury near the indicator muscle you use for testing. The pain or inflammation in that area will interfere with the accuracy of your answers. In this case, try switching to another self-muscle testing technique that's not affected by your injury, ask a friend to perform hetero-muscle testing on you if they are familiar with it, or simply wait until you've healed.

The final scenario where self-muscle testing is not advisable is when you have strong emotions tied to the situation's outcome, for which you seek guidance. You will struggle to remain neutral or objective at a subconscious level and even at a conscious level, and your emotions will likely lead you to favor the answer you want to get. In this case, your emotionally desired outcome will overpower the guidance from your Higher Source.

In these situations, the only solution is to follow the Extensive Approach, which offers steps to help neutralize your emotions, at least temporarily, so you can proceed with your divination session.

Now, let's talk about the actual divination session. A proper divination session has two distinct parts. The first part is preparation, and the second part is your actual connection with the Higher Source of Knowledge and Wisdom to receive guidance and answers.

The preparation phase requires you to set aside focused time to organize your session thoughtfully. This means clearly writing down your questions and reflecting on the potential solutions or answers. When the time comes to connect with your chosen Higher Source, this preparation will make it easier for your Higher Source to point to the best possible option you have written down.

The preparation phase can be done separately and is often the most time-consuming part of the process. While some sessions will be straightforward, others will be more complex and require deep reflection, sometimes taking days or even weeks as you gather and refine your questions and the possible options available to you.

The second part is the actual connection. This is when you tune in to your chosen Higher Source of Knowledge and Wisdom to receive your answers.

Depending on the purpose and importance of your session, I offer three distinct approaches, each with its step-by-step protocol to help you connect with your Higher Source. For simplicity, I've named these approaches the Casual, the Prompt, and the Extensive.

14.2 The Casual Approach

The Casual Approach is used when we want quick answers from our subconscious mind, especially when the question and its answer have little impact on our lives. It is ideal for everyday questions, those times when you're simply seeking a quick answer and nothing important is at stake.

When accessed as a Higher Source of Knowledge and Wisdom, your subconscious mind is always available to you because you spiritually vibrate at the same frequency. It has an opinion on everything, and even if it does not have a definitive answer, it will offer one based on its own reasoning.

In my experience, its answers are often surprisingly precise, even when the questions do not fall strictly within your personal domain, which is typically its area of expertise. If you are wondering why this is the case, I have dedicated an entire chapter to explaining it, so feel free to revisit that section to refresh your understanding.

The **casual approach** requires no elaborate preparation; it just requires three steps: self-muscle test calibration, asking your question, and testing for the answer.

Here is a simple example. Imagine having a late dinner and waking up still feeling full. You remember reading that eating breakfast helps kickstart your metabolism, but you're unsure if it's right for you that particular morning. You decide to consult your subconscious mind as your Higher Source of Knowledge and Wisdom.

Here are the steps:

Step 1: Self-muscle test calibration:

1. "Give me a Yes" (then test)
2. "Give me a No" (then test)

Repeat until you have a clear sense of the strong response "Yes" and the weak response for "No."

Step 2: Ask your question:

Subconscious mind, do you think I should eat breakfast this morning?

Step 3: Self-muscle test: Yes/No

There is actually a fourth step that many of us forget, myself included. That step is to express gratitude. Thank your subconscious mind for its response.

I often skip this out of habit, assuming that since it is part of myself, the gratitude is implied. But honestly, there is no harm in being courteous. Gratitude always strengthens the connection.

14.3 The Prompt Approach

You will want to use this approach when you need answers or, more accurately, recommendations from a Higher Source of Knowledge and Wisdom about issues that matter to you. Your decisions and the actions that follow will have a real impact on your life. In such cases, it is crucial to consult the right Higher Source and receive the answers as they are truly intended, rather than distorted ones.

Distorted answers can happen easily. For example, if you had three cups of coffee earlier, your neuro-muscular system might be overstimulated, making it difficult to relax your indicator muscles. As a result, you might only receive locked or "Yes" answers even when the Higher Source intended to give you a "No" response. On the other hand, if you had consumed alcohol, your muscles might fail to contract properly, leading to constant unlocked or "No" answers.

Emotional involvement can also interfere. If you are deeply attached to a particular outcome or have already made up your mind, even if you ask your Higher Source for guidance, your subconscious or even conscious mind might influence your body to give the answer you want, rather than the intended answer given by the Higher Source.

Both the Prompt and Extensive Approaches include all the necessary steps and techniques to avoid these pitfalls. A key element within them is the **Grounding and Neutralization Technique**.

This technique energetically connects you to Mother Earth, offering numerous benefits. It strengthens your energy field, raises your frequency, and helps you maintain a more objective and neutral perspective on your situation or the issue for which you seek an answer, rather than reacting from personal biases or an overly emotional standpoint. When you ground yourself with Mother

Earth, you can also expect to be nurtured by her and find the support and determination needed to carry out the personal changes you seek.

Due to these numerous benefits, grounding and neutralizing are considered essential spiritual practices. In fact, it is often the foundation upon which other spiritual practices are built. Many of you may already be familiar with grounding techniques and might even have one that you feel comfortable using. If so, continue using yours. If not, you are welcome to use the one I provide, which can be found in Appendix C.

The main reason to choose the Prompt Approach is when you are short on time. The only difference between the Prompt Approach and the Extensive Approach is that the latter incorporates the 8th Gateway Technique, which adds more time to the process.

However, to safely skip the 8th Gateway Technique, you must genuinely feel physically healthy, emotionally balanced, and happy, maintain a positive outlook on life, and have a clean and strong energetic and etheric body; then you are likely vibrating at a higher frequency. If you meet these conditions, it means you are vibrating at a high frequency and should not experience difficulty accessing any of the Higher Sources of Knowledge and Wisdom.

If you do not feel this way, it is more likely you will encounter difficulties in connecting. In that case, you will need to perform the 8th Gateway Technique, which will elevate your frequency to the required level and beyond!

Here is the protocol for the Prompt Approach:

Step 1: Ensure there are no reasons that would contraindicate self-muscle testing. Several factors can negatively impact the process, and they are fully explained in Chapter 14.1.

Step 2: Prepare for your divination session.

- Do you have your written questions and their potential solutions or answers ready in front of you?

- Did you choose a time when you know you will not be disturbed?
- Did you put your phone on silent mode and preferably leave it in another room?
- Are your room temperature and body temperature comfortable? If your fingers are too cold or too hot and sweaty, you may receive distorted answers, so ensure you are physically comfortable.

Step 3: Hydrate with pure water if your body needs it.

Step 4: Start your session with Deep Conscious Harmonious Breathing. See Appendix A.

Step 5: After a few minutes, proceed with the Grounding and Neutralization Technique. See Appendix B.

(If you are following the Extensive Approach, this is where you also perform the 8th Gateway Technique. See Appendix C)

Step 6: Say the following affirmation three times, feeling it deeply and knowing it to be true:

I am one with all that is

I am one with all that is

I am one with all that is

Step 7: Set a clear intention to align with your desired Higher Source of Knowledge and Wisdom.

Declare:

"I now choose to integrate with my...(Higher Self, the Akashic Records, or another Higher Source)... for the purpose of receiving truthful answers free from personal preference or past experience. So be it. So be it. So be it."

Step 8: Calibrate your self-muscle testing.

1. **"Give me a Yes"** (then test)

2. **"Give me a No"** (then test)

Repeat until you have a clear sense of the strong response "Yes" and the weak response for "No." You can then proceed with two more calibration questions.

- **Is my name ________?**
- **Is my birth date ________?**

If your answers were correct, proceed to Step 9.

Step 9: Ask your questions and receive your answers through self-muscle testing.

Your first question should be:
"Have I successfully connected with my intended Higher Source?"

About 80 percent of the time, you will have successfully made the connection and can proceed.

If you happen to fall into the 20 percent where the connection is not made, especially if you are in a lower vibratory state, you will need to perform the 8th Gateway Technique. If you do not have time for it, reschedule your divination session for another time.

If you are connecting with any of the following Higher Sources: Higher Self, Over Soul, or the Akashic Records, you need to always include in your answers the option 'Cannot answer'.

If this option is given, ask: "When can I ask again? Never? (test), After one week? (test), after three weeks (test), after two months (test), and so on, until you receive a positive confirmation." Don't forget to record your answer!

Step 10: When you have completed your divination session, remember to express your gratitude.

14.4 The Extensive Approach

All Higher Sources of Knowledge and Wisdom described in this book, with the exception of your subconscious mind, operate at a higher vibratory frequency than your own. If the gap in frequency is too wide, it may become difficult or even impossible to connect with and access those Higher Sources.

When you are physically healthy, emotionally balanced, happy, maintain a positive outlook on life, and your energetic and etheric bodies are clean and strong, then you are likely vibrating at a higher frequency. This also means that it is very likely that you will have no issues accessing any of the Higher Sources of Knowledge and Wisdom.

If you are not in that optimal state, however, you will need to raise your frequency. From my personal experience, as well as that of my students, performing the 8th Gateway Technique has always been sufficient. The only difference between the Prompt Approach and the Extensive Approach is the addition of the 8th Gateway Technique between steps 5 and 6.

Protocol for the Extensive Approach:

- **Steps 1 to 5:** Same as the Prompt Approach
- **Perform the 8th Gateway Technique (APPENDIX C)**
- **Steps 7 to 10:** Continue with the remaining steps from the Prompt Approach

CHAPTER 15

What to Do Next

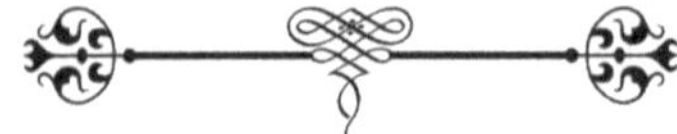

If you have read this book up to this point, then you are now familiar with all the tools and procedures needed to conduct a successful divination session using your chosen Higher Source of Knowledge and Wisdom, along with self-muscle testing.

The next step is to become truly proficient with these tools and procedures so that you no longer need to refer back to this book for guidance. Your self-muscle testing should eventually become second nature. To the best of my knowledge, there is only one way to reach that level of mastery, and that is through consistent practice. Practice really does make perfect.

This is the same advice I shared with all of my students at the end of every seminar.

I recommend that you practice your top two self-muscle testing techniques consistently for the next three weeks. Keep it casual! During this time, test anything and everything around you. There is nothing in your surroundings that cannot be tested.

Look at the wall next to you and ask:

- Is the color of the wall white? Yes or no
- Is the color of the wall black? Yes or no
- Is the color of the wall pink? Yes or no

Look at a nearby car and ask:

- Is the color of this car yellow? Yes or no

- Is the color of this car green? Yes or no
- Is the color of this car brown? Yes or no

Now ask yourself:

- Am I living in Africa? Yes or no
- Am I a woman? Yes or no
- Am I a man? Yes or no
- Do I come from planet Pluto? Yes or no
- Do I come from planet Jupiter? Yes or no

I hope you see my point. Finding questions for self-muscle testing is a piece of cake!

Please remember to always begin with the basic calibration steps:

1. "Give me a Yes" (then test)
2. "Give me a No" (then test)

In truth, all of the examples I listed above are calibration questions.

It is also important to always pause for about two seconds after asking your question before performing the test. If you ask and immediately test, and you get a weak response, you may find yourself wondering whether it was actually a "No" or whether your muscles simply did not have time to respond. Then you repeat the test and start to second-guess the outcome.

What else should you do?

You need to become comfortable and proficient with the three key techniques introduced in the Prompt and Extensive Approaches. These are:

- Appendix A: Deep Conscious Harmonious Breathing
- Appendix B: Grounding and Neutralization Technique
- Appendix C: The 8th Gateway Technique

Please find time to practice these as well. They offer many powerful benefits, especially for those serious about developing their psychic potential. However, please do not attempt to connect with any Higher Source of Knowledge and Wisdom to ask questions until you feel confident in your self-muscle testing technique.

...My Higher Self just cut in and asked, “What about me?”

“What about you?” I replied (Apparently, he did not get my joke)

In all seriousness, if you wish to deepen your communication with your Higher Self, then I encourage you to practice the additional techniques shared in the chapter dedicated to the Higher Self.

At the same time, as you practice and grow, make sure to begin preparing for your first official divination session. After all, this is the reason you are investing your time and energy.

And here is the best part: self-muscle testing is like learning to ride a bicycle. Once you learn it well, it stays with you for life!

CHAPTER 16

What Is One Question You Should Include in Your First Divination Session Using the Prompt or Extensive Approach?

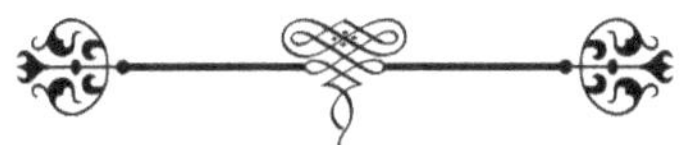

In my opinion, during your first divination session—likely with your Higher Self or the Akashic Records—you should also ask which self-muscle testing technique or finger combination should be your primary method, and which should be your secondary. This is especially important if you have more than three techniques scoring 10 out of 10. Your Higher Source knows which method produces the most accurate results for you.

If that is the case, make a list of the techniques and ask the following question:

Dear Higher Self or Akashic Records, please indicate which of the following self-muscle testing techniques or finger combinations should be my primary technique.

Then ask:

Which one should I use as my secondary technique?

"You are not a drop in the ocean. You are the entire ocean in a drop."

— Rumi

CHAPTER 17

Affirmations That Will Fortify Your Divination Tool

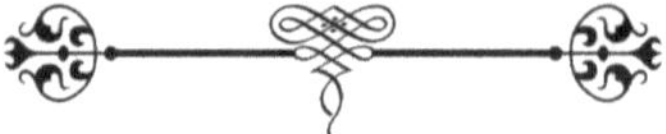

Here are two affirmations that will strengthen both your self-muscle testing ability and your connection to Higher Sources of Knowledge and Wisdom:

- **Every day, in every way, my ability to connect to Higher Sources of Knowledge and Wisdom is getting better and better.**
- **Every day, in every way, my self-muscle testing ability is getting better and better.**

All affirmations are best read in the morning before getting out of bed and at night before going to sleep. For this reason, it is helpful to have them written down and placed by your bedside.

"As your conscious mind rests, the gate to the infinite opens. Let your affirmations become the whispers that shape your destiny."

— George C. Georgiou

CHAPTER 18

Troubleshooting Scenarios

18.1 I am being denied an answer about a crucial matter

"I have a personal question on a serious issue, and it is vital that I receive an answer, either from my Higher Self or the Akashic Records, as they are the most qualified to address this particular concern. I followed the Extensive approach and confirmed that I was connected to my Higher Self. I then asked if it was appropriate to receive an answer to this specific question and was told, 'Not at this time.' I continued with other questions that I had prepared and received clear answers for each. However, the same response came through when I returned to my original question.

While still in my meditative state, I thanked my Higher Self and shifted to the Akashic Records. I confirmed the connection, but once again, when I asked about my pressing question, I received the same response: 'Not at this time.'

This question feels like a matter of life or death. I am cornered. Waiting until tomorrow might be too late. Why am I being denied the guidance I so urgently need?"

Answer:

The answer is simple. Each Higher Source has its own set of rules and conditions regarding the release of information, which are explained in more detail in their respective chapters.

That said, you still have multiple options available to you.

First, the response 'Not at this time' can mean a few things. Most obviously, it could mean that events are still unfolding and the best course of action is not yet clear. In such cases, it is wise to ask again at a later time. You can even specify, asking when would be a good time to try again: tomorrow, the next day, in a week, and so on.

Also, make sure to include "Do nothing at this moment" as one of the possible answers. This option was recommended to me many times, and every time I followed it, it proved to be the wisest course of action.

If circumstances are such that tomorrow will be too late, then it is likely that you are being guided to face this situation on your own without external input. This is not a punishment, nor a sign that your Higher Sources are being unkind or dismissive. Rather, it suggests that you are engaged in a meaningful learning experience. In such moments, it is vital that you take your own course of action. Trust that whatever the outcome may be, it is part of your growth. You did your best under pressure, you gained experience, and now you move forward. This is the nature of life on Earth.

Now, having said this, here are a few alternative solutions!

Option One: Try using the Casual approach. The subconscious mind always has an opinion, even if it lacks complete data. It can still provide surprisingly accurate answers based on its own reasoning and resources. I have discussed this in detail in Chapter 10.1, which you may want to revisit.

Option Two: Rephrase your question. It may sound simple, but I have found this technique very effective. Try changing the emphasis or clarifying your intentions.

Option Three: This one is a bit ironic. I once asked the Akashic Records for advice on how to get an answer from another higher source when they deny access. And yes, they gave me an answer!

Use a variation of the Prompt approach. Everything remains the same except for Step 7. Instead of declaring:

"I now choose to integrate with my... (the Akashic Records or another Higher Source)... for the purpose of receiving truthful answers, free from personal preference or past experience. So be it. So be it. So be it."

You say:

"I am one with all that is. I access and receive the right answers, free from personal preference or past experience, drawn from wherever truth resides. So be it. So be it. So be it."

And there you have it.

18.2 I do not know which Higher Source holds the answer to my question

Answer: The Akashic Records have access to all answers, but they may choose not to share them for reasons already discussed. In this case, refer back to the guidance offered in section 18.1.

18.3 I am too emotional to ask about a particular issue

"I want to ask about something deeply important, but I get emotional just thinking about it. I feel strongly about what I want the answer to be, which makes it difficult to receive an objective response from a Higher Source. What should I do?"

Answer: Try one or more of the following:

- Use the Extensive approach
- Work specifically with the Akashic Records
- Ask from a third-person perspective. For example, say: "I now wish to ask some questions about... (insert your name)... born on... (insert your birth date)... and I have his or her permission."

These steps greatly improve your chances of receiving the intended response from the Higher Source.

18.4 I cannot even get the calibration questions right, even after switching to my second-best self-muscle testing technique

Answer: This could be due to several factors, such as dehydration, illness, or toxins in the body. See pages 103–104 for more details. Whatever the cause, take a break from self-muscle testing for at least one day.

18.5 It is not any of the above reasons, and the problem continues the next day. I am even getting opposite answers. What happened? Why did I lose my touch?

Here are some possibilities:

- With finger techniques, your fingers must form a circle. An oval shape will yield false negatives.
- Overusing the same muscles or testing method can cause fatigue of the indicator muscles and distort results.
- You might be skipping the two-second pause rule after asking a question. Always allow time for the energy to align.
- The amount of force used on the indicator muscle should be consistent and relatively gentle. Avoid using excessive strength. The goal is to detect a lock or unlock response, rather than applying sheer force.
- Perform the Deep Conscious Harmonious Breathing exercise (Appendix A), the Grounding and Neutralization Technique (Appendix B), or the 8th Gateway Technique (Appendix C) to realign emotional, etheric, and energetic bodies.
- On a physical level, you might be too tired or emotionally depleted.

Also, consider testing for deficiencies in the following:

Vitamins:

- Vitamin B1 (Thiamine) Yes/No
- Vitamin B6 (Pyridoxine) Yes/No
- Vitamin B12 (Cobalamin) Yes/No
- Vitamin B9 (Folate) Yes/No
- Vitamin D Yes/No
- Vitamin E Yes/No

Minerals:

- Magnesium Yes/No
- Calcium Yes/No
- Potassium Yes/No
- Zinc Yes/No
- Iron Yes/No
- Copper Yes/No

Herbs:

- Rhodiola Yes/No
- Ashwagandha Yes/No

You may need to consider a condition known only in the domain of applied kinesiology/kinesiology, referred to as "Switching." This is when the body's nervous system becomes functionally disorganized, disrupting its ability to process information. Initially identified by Drs. Goodheart, Walther, and Ferreri, this condition can produce inaccurate or reversed responses during muscle testing. This must be corrected before proceeding.

The causes may include those listed in Chapter 14.1, as well as traumas (both physical and emotional) and even spinal misalignments. To address this, I have developed a set of simple exercises that have consistently helped restore proper function.

Start by sitting comfortably. Roll your eyes in a circle a few times clockwise, then counterclockwise. It does not matter whether your eyes are open or closed.

Place your right hand flat on the top of your head. With gentle pressure, move your hand as if you are drawing five clockwise circles and then five counterclockwise circles. Repeat with your left hand.

Finally, perform any cross-crawl exercise of your choice for 30 to 45 seconds. These movements enhance communication between the right and left hemispheres of the brain.

Cross-crawl involves coordinated movement between opposite limbs, such as the right arm and left leg. Examples include Cross-Crawl Marching, Standing Cross-Body Toe Touches, Bird-Dog, Twisting Toe Touches, and swimming.

Look up these exercises online to ensure proper technique. Most can be done anywhere, even in your living room.

I recommend performing this routine periodically to help keep you balanced and fine-tuned. Why wait until you are completely out of sync before taking action?

"It always seems impossible until it's done."

— Nelson Mandela

CHAPTER 19

General Applications Of Self-Muscle Testing for Divination

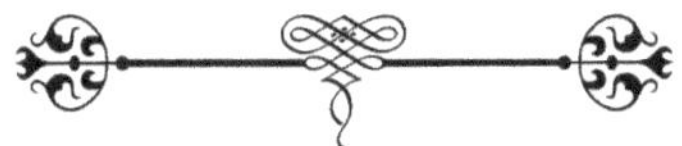

Thanks to the second and third core principles, "Universal Application" and "Connection with Spiritual Sources," which you'll find in Chapter 7 of this book, the potential uses of self-muscle testing are infinite, or as I like to say, limited only by your imagination.

I'm going to prove it by sharing a few pages packed with the wildest, strangest, and most unexpected ways I've used self-muscle testing over the years. Why? Because I want to ignite your imagination so you're not confined by it. And once I'm done with these examples, I'm not stopping there! I've decided to bring in a guest author, known as ChatGPT 3.5, to offer even more ideas and further expand your horizons. But guess what? That's still not the end! What does that mean exactly? Great question. I might be hinting at the advanced applications coming up next, designed to take your skills and possibilities to the next level!

But for now, let me begin with a personal story that led to a discovery that completely blew my mind, and I'm sure it will for you too. Around the year 2020, I believed I was living a healthy life. I was content with my vegetarian lifestyle, practiced daily meditation, and occasionally enjoyed long walks along the seaside promenade of my hometown, Limassol, Cyprus. Sure, I was under a lot of stress at the time, and there were many aspects of my life I wasn't thrilled about, but that's just life in a big city in the Western world, and something I had grown accustomed to.

Around that time, I began experiencing symptoms that reminded me of an earlier, difficult period in my life, and that scared me. I started gaining weight, struggled with poor memory and brain fog, insomnia returned with a vengeance, and depression slowly crept back in.

So, naturally, I turned to my Higher Self for guidance. My first question went straight to my biggest fear: "Is there an ET race visiting me again and messing with me?"

He reassured me that this was not the case, and those experiences wouldn't be repeated, as agreed. I sighed in relief and asked the next big question: "Why am I having all these health issues?"

The answer shocked me.

Higher Self: It's your so-called supplements that are negatively affecting your health.

Author's Side Note: Let me explain. After I turned forty, I fell into a habit. Whenever I read about a vitamin or herb with special health benefits, I would buy it and add it to a special shelf in my office. Then, throughout the day, I would do self-muscle testing and pop a few pills based on what I thought my body needed.

So, at that moment, I protested, "But I'm asking my body and then I'm giving it what it needs!"

Higher Self: No, you think you are, but you're not.

Author: What do you mean? Please explain.

Higher Self: This is what you do: you look at a bottle on your shelf, you read the label, and ask, "Do I need to take B Complex right now?" You get a yes.

Then you ask, "Do I need one tablet?" You get a yes. "Do I need two?" You get a no. So, you think your body needs one 400mg capsule of B vitamins? Correct?

Author: Yes, that's exactly what I do. Is it wrong?

Higher Self: The mistake comes next. You reach out, grab that bottle, take the capsule, and swallow it, believing you're giving your body exactly what it asked for. But what's actually inside that capsule is a mix of synthetic substances and not that vitamin. These factory-made vitamins differ from those found in nature. They're different, and they affect your body negatively. Did you know that the paint used on one of those capsules causes cancerous cell reactions within your liver? Did you know that many of the transparent gelatin capsules that store the supplement contain viruses and bacteria of animal origin, which in turn activate your immune system and contribute to your fatigue?

Author: Oh, shit.

Higher Self: Yes, dear. For this reason, we recommend more accurate methods for self-testing your supplements. You should be testing the energy of the actual contents in the bottle. Let's go back to the B Complex example. Say you test and get a yes, that you need more B vitamins in your system. Up to this point, it's all good; we have no doubts about that, but there should be another step as follows. Place the bottle on your lap or hold it in your hand for a few seconds. This allows your aura to scan the contents energetically. Then ask, "Is the content of this bottle beneficial to my health?" and test again. This time around, you may notice a completely different answer.

Let me give you another example. You consume ascorbic acid, believing you are taking vitamin C, but this is far from the truth. Vitamin C is not a single molecule but a complex nutritional matrix made up of various atoms, enzymes, trace minerals, and other compounds. Your scientists have yet to fully identify or replicate all the components that make up vitamin C as it is found in nature, which is why synthetic versions fall short to a degree that the end product is actually harmful to you.

That conversation was a major wake-up call. After the session, I stormed into my office and tested all my supplements. Most of them tested as not beneficial, and I threw them away on the spot. I must have tossed out 500 euros' worth of supplements in less than five minutes.

The few that passed the test were unencapsulated minerals. I also had some herbal supplements in capsules that didn't pass, but I ran an experiment. I unscrewed the capsules, emptied the herbal powder into a separate container, and tested again. This time, the herbal powder was tested beneficial on its own.

Since then, I take my favorite herbs like Rhodiola and Ashwagandha, without their capsules, mix them with half a glass of water, add half a spoon of raw honey, stir well, and drink the mixture.

I also became more intentional when shopping. I tested everything by asking just two questions: "Is this fresh?" and "Would this be beneficial for me right now?" Also, once a week, I started driving to a farmer's market where I knew the produce was fresh and worth the extra trouble.

After making these changes, I felt like I was thirty again within a month.

Staying with the physical body, there are obviously many more things you can ask. The best approach here is the casual. Your subconscious mind is intimately aware of your body, from its metabolic activities and bodily functions to its DNA and genes. This is precisely why I chose to remove the chapter on DNA, which is another massive internal database. Trust me, after removing it, the book feels much lighter, and you are not missing anything. Your subconscious can answer any question that might have been directed to your DNA just as accurately.

Just by calibrating your divination tool, you can directly ask your subconscious if you are allergic to something, suffering from a particular condition, or likely to develop one. You can then ask what lifestyle changes you should make to prevent it.

Example questions:

- Am I allergic to dairy products?
- Do I have type 2 diabetes?
- Am I currently vitamin D deficient?
- Am I prone to high blood pressure?
- Should I stop eating processed sugar?

- Is regular aerobic (or strength, or flexibility, or balance, or functional fitness) exercise important for preventing illness in my case?
- Would reducing my caffeine intake improve my health?
- Should I avoid gluten to prevent autoimmune issues?
- Which of the following foods worsen my headaches?

If you are considering treatment and have several options, you can ask which one or which combination would be best for you.

More practical examples:

-Planning a holiday?

Narrowed it down to three places, but still can't decide? Ask your subconscious or Higher Self. They might know something you don't about those destinations and what awaits you there!

- Choosing a house:
"Subconscious mind, of all the houses we visited today, which one had the best energy for me or us? And which one had the second-best?"

- Designing an exercise program:
"Subconscious mind, please help me select the exercises my body needs most right now."

- Improving life in general:
"What should I reduce or remove from my life to make it better?"
"What should I increase or add to my life to improve it?"

- Choosing events to attend:

Author's Side Note:

I've been to too many overhyped workshops that failed to deliver, complete wastes of time and money! Some even cost me thousands when I factored in travel and accommodation. More than once, I ignored clear warnings from Higher Sources of Knowledge and Wisdom because the promises sounded so

irresistible. Never again. These days, if I get a "No," I accept it without hesitation or regret!

“Akashic Records, Subconscious, or Higher Self, will this retreat, workshop, or seminar really be as good as it sounds, and will it be worth it for me?” (Especially with this one, please remember the 2-second pause rule before testing)

- Buying a car:
"Which of these three cars will best reflect a professional, trustworthy, yet laid-back image?"

- What to wear for special occasions:

Letting your subconscious choose your wardrobe for a special occasion is always a good idea. Why? Because your subconscious picks up, records, and analyzes the first impressions and reactions of the people you meet while wearing those clothes, making it the ultimate expert database. To use this method, lay out several different outfits on your bed and test each one.

- Job interview:
  “Subconscious mind, which clothes should I wear today to send the message I am the one for the job?”

- Business meeting:
  “Subconscious mind, what outfit will make them think I have been working extra hard since our last meeting?” 😊

- Presentation:
  “Subconscious mind, what should I wear today to convey authority and creativity?”

- Hot date:
  “Subconscious mind, which outfit says I am yours, baby?” 😊

- Just-friends date:
  “Subconscious mind, which outfit clearly says nothing will happen, we’re just good friends?” 😊

- Family gathering:
  "Subconscious mind, which outfit will convince everyone that I've finally pulled myself together?" 😊
- Attracting good vibes:
  "Subconscious mind, what should I wear today to attract happiness and good luck into my life?"

Continuing with the casual approach, your subconscious mind is not only familiar with your physical state, but it also knows the current condition of your emotional, mental, spiritual, and energetic bodies.

Some of the example questions I have prepared are simple and direct, designed to provide clear yes-or-no answers. Others are crafted to encourage a bit of self-exploration before you ask, prompting deeper reflection and insight.

Have fun with the process and enjoy the journey of self-discovery!

Emotional Body:

- Which emotion am I deficient in that needs to be felt and integrated?
- Which emotion am I repressing right now that is making me sick?
- Am I emotionally entangled with someone else's energy?
- Is an unhealed emotional wound attracting certain patterns to my life?
- Am I emotionally aligned with my soul's path?
- Is a past emotional event influencing my present relationships?
- Which suppressed emotion is manifesting physically?

Spiritual Body:

- Am I currently in alignment with my soul purpose?

- Is my soul contract being fulfilled in this life stage?
- How many permanent guides do I have?
- How many special assignment guides do I currently have?
- Is a past-life issue creating resistance in my current spiritual path?

Mental Body:

- Which thought am I deficient in?
- Which thought is making me sick?
- Am I holding a belief that no longer serves me?
- Is there a limiting belief affecting my health or well-being?
- Is this thought serving my highest good?
- Is a collective belief influencing my personal mindset?

Energetic Body:

- Which of my chakras, meridians, or Nadis needs my attention?
- Which chakra is currently underactive or overactive?
- Is my aura compromised or leaking energy?
- Do I have a spirit attachment?
- Am I connected to another person energetically?

****

I also asked ChatGPT 3.5 to co-author a few pages with me, which it gladly accepted. My aim here is to provide you with an additional 60 ideas that utilize self-muscle testing, demonstrating that you can ask anything you desire and make your imagination limitless!

Dear ChatGPT:

I am interested in self-muscle testing as a divination tool in our lives. Could you please provide me with 60 applications of self-muscle testing for divination purposes, categorized as ordinary, less ordinary, and supernatural?

<u>20 Ordinary Applications of Self-muscle Testing</u>

1. Locating underground water sources (for wells or irrigation)
2. Finding underground pipes or cables
3. Detecting septic tanks or utility lines
4. Testing for geopathic stress zones in homes
5. Choosing optimal locations for planting trees or crops
6. Checking the energy of food or water (e.g. for vitality or compatibility)
7. Finding lost items like keys or wallets
8. Assessing compatibility with supplements or medications
9. Testing for allergies or sensitivities
10. Checking EMF levels and identifying safer zones in the home
11. Testing soil quality or moisture content for gardening
12. Choosing optimal driving routes (based on intuition)
13. Determining which groceries are energetically best for you
14. Locating the best area to place your bed or desk in a room
15. Testing the potency of vitamins or supplements
16. Determining energetic compatibility with pets
17. Selecting household cleaning products with fewer harmful effects

18. Verifying the quality of tap vs. bottled water
19. Finding the source of mold or environmental stress in a house
20. Choosing between job offers or business decisions

20 Less Ordinary Applications of Self-muscle Testing

1. Choosing ideal dates for important events
2. Locating lost pets
3. Finding misplaced or hidden documents
4. Testing chakra balance or energy field strength
5. Selecting optimal healing modalities (e.g. Reiki, herbs, sound therapy)
6. Detecting energetic blockages in buildings
7. Detecting non-beneficial energies from a space
8. Selecting beneficial crystals or gemstones for personal use
9. Determining past-life influences on present situations
10. Enhancing intuition by confirming inner guidance
11. Navigating energy fields at sacred or historic sites
12. Determining if a property or house has a beneficial energy signature
13. Locating areas of high life-force energy (for meditation or healing)
14. Finding which mantra or affirmation holds the highest resonance
15. Detecting personal energetic attachments (cords, contracts, agreements)
16. Assessing alignment with a spiritual path or teacher
17. Choosing the most aligned location for travel or relocation

18. Testing the vibration of books, courses, or teachings before engaging
19. Receiving yes/no answers to spiritual or emotional dilemmas
20. Fine-tuning personal rituals or sacred space arrangements

20 Supernatural Applications of Self-muscle Testing

1. Communicating with spirit guides or Higher Self
2. Accessing Akashic Records for soul-level answers
3. Identifying curses, entity attachments, or spiritual interference
4. Locating portals, ley lines, or energy vortices
5. Confirming the identity of a spirit
6. Identifying karmic imprints or ancestral patterns
7. Tracking astral activity or dream-based information
8. Facilitating interdimensional communication
9. Identifying the presence and location of interdimensional beings
10. Checking for the presence of ancestral spirits or guides
11. Measuring soul frequency or spiritual advancement
12. Identifying locations of past-life trauma
13. Accessing future soul contracts or mission updates
14. Determining which spiritual gifts are currently active or dormant
15. Pinpointing the origin of psychic attacks or energetic drains
16. Mapping out chakra systems beyond the traditional seven
17. Identifying karmic entanglements with other souls
18. Pinpointing the presence of portals or energetic gateways

19. Determining the alignment of your spirit with cosmic cycles

20. Locating soul fragments for retrieval and integration

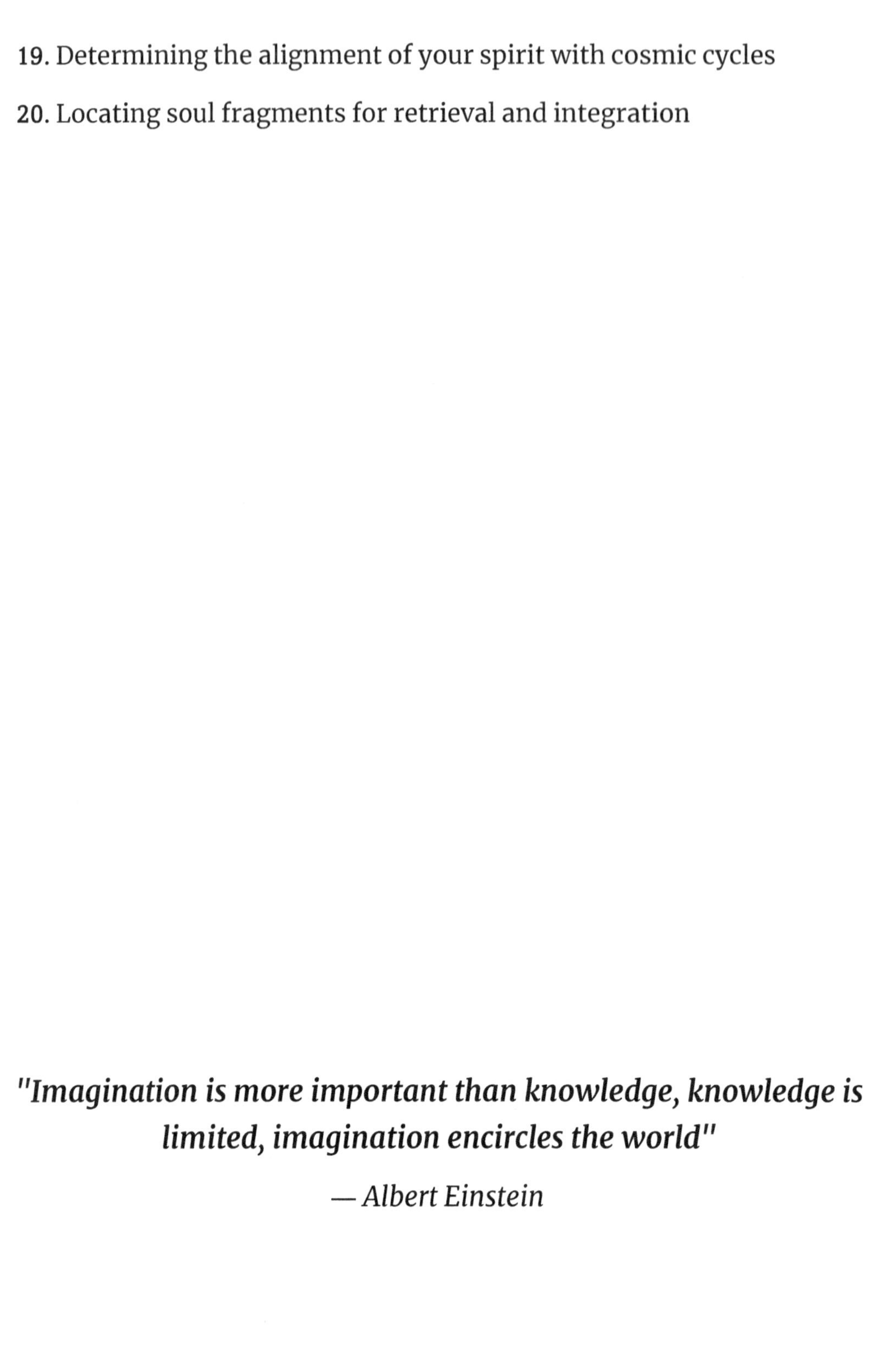

"Imagination is more important than knowledge, knowledge is limited, imagination encircles the world"

— Albert Einstein

CHAPTER 20

Advanced Applications Of Self-Muscle Testing for Divination

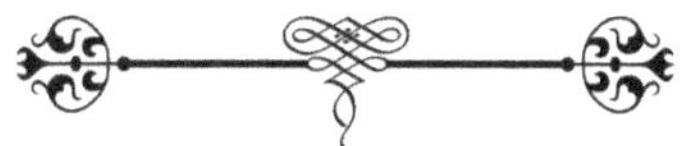

20.1 Surrogate Muscle Testing

This type of muscle testing involves using a substitute or surrogate, someone who is physically healthy and agrees to have their muscles tested on behalf of another person who is unable to undergo muscle testing themselves due to physical or mental limitations.

This technique is especially useful for obtaining information from infants, young children, comatose patients, and others living with severe health impairments. I also include animals in this group, as they, too, are unable to express what they are feeling or where it hurts. Many pet owners have shared their frustration and heartbreak with me, explaining how veterinarians often resort to a series of costly and general tests, simply because the actual cause remains hidden.

To conduct surrogate muscle testing, you will need the following: a person proficient in hetero muscle testing and/or self-muscle testing, the surrogate person, the person or animal from whom we need the information, and finally, a connector. A connector is an item that connects the person from whom we need answers and the surrogate person, typically a string, preferably made of cotton. In case of an animal, you will simply use its leash. The leash will be connected to the animal and held by its owner, as shown in the picture below.

If you do not have a string of any kind, you can improvise. For example, use a pair of trousers belonging to the person you want to get answers from. Tie one leg of the trousers to their wrist and the other leg to the wrist of the surrogate.

There are two ways this can be done. The first, which requires a constructor, is the traditional way, and the other, which doesn't require one, is a more modern version. As far as I know, I haven't seen it in any other kinesiology books, so I may have come up with this idea myself, who knows!

In the image below, the author uses the pet owner as a surrogate. After establishing a mental and energetic connection with both the owner and the dog, the author asks a series of questions and performs muscle testing on the pet owner. The pet owner's arm serves as the indicator arm, providing yes or no answers on behalf of the dog.

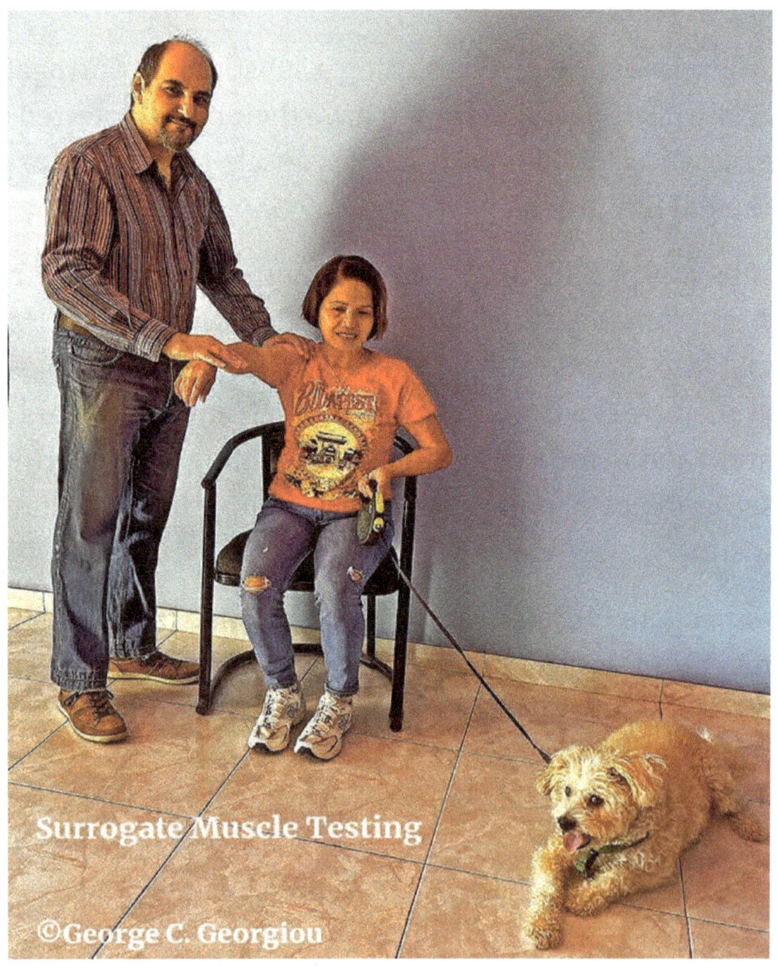

Question: What do you mean by "establishing a mental and energetic connection with both the owner and the dog"?

Answer: This is an important step because if it is not done, or not done correctly, you may end up receiving answers that pertain to the body of the surrogate rather than that of the animal or the incapacitated person from whom the answers are intended to come.

Each kinesiologist has their own approach, shaped by their education and experience. Here is what I do:

Silently, I say: "I now wish to expand my aura to include those of the person next to me and that of the dog." (Wait 5 seconds)

"I now wish to connect with the dog for the purpose of receiving answers concerning his or her health." (Wait 5 seconds)

That is all.

I then proceed to calibrate the pet owner's indicator arm by asking some simple questions such as "Is your name...(correct name)?", "Is your name...(incorrect name)?" and "Is your dog's name...?" This step is particularly important, not only for calibrating our tool to ensure we obtain the correct answers, but also because the pet owner may be unfamiliar with muscle testing. This process helps demonstrate how it works.

Question: What do you mean by 'asking a series of questions and performing muscle testing on the pet owner'?

Answer: In this example, we are trying to locate the root cause of a symptom, and we have no idea what is causing it. We may be dealing with a quadriplegic or an animal, but the process is the same.

We begin by asking which bodily system is responsible for the symptom. This involves asking the following eleven questions:

- Is the root cause of (enter the symptom) coming from the circulatory system?
- Is the root cause of (enter the symptom) coming from the respiratory system?

- Is the root cause of (enter the symptom) coming from the digestive system?
- Is the root cause of (enter the symptom) coming from the nervous system?
- Is the root cause of (enter the symptom) coming from the muscular system?
- Is the root cause of (enter the symptom) coming from the skeletal system?
- Is the root cause of (enter the symptom) coming from the endocrine system?
- Is the root cause of (enter the symptom) coming from the reproductive system?
- Is the root cause of (enter the symptom) coming from the urinary system?
- Is the root cause of (enter the symptom) coming from the immune system?
- Is the root cause of (enter the symptom) coming from the integumentary system? (This includes skin, hair, nails, fur, feathers, or scales.)

20.2 But There's Something Better Than Surrogate Testing

Here is a surprise for you.

I have never used surrogate muscle testing in my life, except for the purpose of writing this book. I simply wanted to be thorough and demonstrate the process. However, I have always employed a more modern approach, where you can access the information you need without requiring a surrogate or any kind of connector.

Even when clients asked me to perform surrogate testing on their comatose loved ones or their animals, I explained that I do not need to be physically present. At first, they are skeptical. However, when I tell them that I can connect with their loved ones through the Akashic Records or their Higher Self, and that I can provide ten times more information than if I were there in person, and offer them written instructions and recommendations, they are not only satisfied but also very excited.

This modern method offers two different approaches.

The first one involves sitting next to the person or animal from whom you wish to receive information. You then establish a mental and energetic connection as described earlier.

I would proceed by calibrating my divination tool and, if the client is a person, I would also ask permission from their Higher Self. I have also noticed that the answers tend to be stronger or clearer when there is some physical contact.

For example, if it is a person, I like to sit beside them at knee level, with my bent knee placed horizontally on the bed so it lightly touches their leg. If it is an animal, the contact depends on their size. In the picture below, you can see that part of the dog's body is resting on my thigh while I perform the muscle testing.

The second method involves using a photo of the person or animal you want to gather information about. It is crucial that the photo is very recent, ideally taken within the last 24 hours. This helps ensure you are tuning into their current and most accurate energetic state. Along with the photo, you will also need the person's full name and date of birth. This information is necessary to connect with the correct individual and request permission from their Higher Self to access their information. You might be surprised how often access is denied.

This usually happens when a guardian forgets to inform the incapacitated person that they've contacted someone like me, for example, who will be snooping around their energy for their own well-being. It drives me crazy when I finally find the time to tune in, only to be blocked entirely. Then I had to check in with the client, and, surprise, surprise, I was right! Most of the time, they offer a weak excuse, like, "Oh, I forgot they can still hear everything," as if that makes it any better.

And that's it, a whole toolkit of ideas and options, no matter where you are or what you're dealing with. Feels kind of amazing, doesn't it? You no longer need to rely on people like me, sit on waiting lists, or spend a fortune just to get some answers. In my opinion, the training in this book, and becoming proficient in self-muscle testing for divination purposes, is hands down one of the smartest moves and best investments you can make for your personal growth and peace of mind.

"You are confined only by the walls you build yourself."

— Andrew Murphy

CHAPTER 21

Love, Relationships, and the Truth Behind the Million-Dollar Question

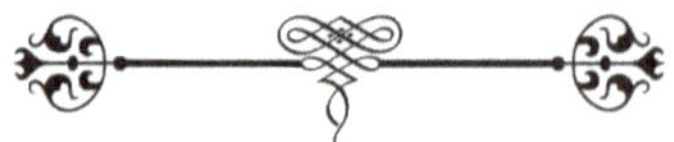

The fascination with love, soulmates, and relationship dynamics has been evident in both the workshops I used to lead and my private sessions as an Akashic Records consultant. In fact, around 70 percent of my one-on-one sessions focused on a single main concern: relationships. At the end of every workshop, when I opened the floor for questions, about 80

percent of the time was dedicated to these topics.

My workshops typically lasted a day and a half, starting on Saturday morning and concluding officially by noon on Sunday. But the relationship questions just kept coming. Many times, I would not leave until after 1:30 p.m., completely drained of energy. 😟

People asked me everything under the sun:
"Will the Akashic Records answer this?"
"Will my Higher Self answer this?"
"Should I wait for someone from the same Oversoul?"
"What if they are not my soulmate?"
"Can I test whether we'll get divorced in the future?"
"Which Higher Source is best for this question?"

Is this situation the result of past-life karma?

By now, I hope you've become comfortable working with the appropriate Higher Source of Knowledge and Wisdom, and that you can use your preferred self-muscle testing method to get reliable answers.

That said, I want to address the million-dollar question I'm asked all the time directly. The answer is straightforward, but it deserves some deeper context.

The question goes like this:
"I asked my Higher Self, and it said that he or she is not my soulmate... but I love them deeply. What should I do?"

Here is my answer:

Do not let that stop you. If you truly love someone and the relationship feels good and enriching, that is already something powerful and worth cherishing.

Soulmates can indeed have dream-like or fairy-tale marriages that last over 50 years, the kind that is always in harmony and where the partners cannot imagine living apart. But this is just one rare possibility. The truth is that soulmates are not immune to heartbreak. They can argue, drift apart, and even experience painful breakups or messy divorces. On the other hand, people who are not officially soulmates can build relationships that are solid, kind, passionate, and lifelong.

Let me explain why all these scenarios are possible. First, I want to refresh your memory with the following excerpts from Chapter 11.1 titled "Oversoul Collective" in this book:

'Each Oversoul is a collective consciousness composed of 144,000 individual souls, or team members.'

'These 144,000 individual souls that comprise one Oversoul share a profound connection and carry identical vibrational frequencies. That is why when two such souls happen to meet randomly, an instant and often 'unexplainable' emotional connection is felt between them, accompanied by the feeling of Deja Vu.

Both of those feelings are justifiable as they most likely met in one or more past/future lifetimes, exchanged experiences, and created karma between them, further complicating their connection as seen from a human perspective.'

Based on this information, it means that you do not have just one soul mate but 143,999. If you happen to find one another, the type of relationship you will share will depend on your joint karma and any life contracts you made before incarnating.

From my experience, both personal and as an Akashic Records consultant, when two people are soul mates, everything tends to feel more emotionally intense. There is often a powerful and passionate love, but there are also cases where soul mates experience strong disagreements and heated arguments. The connection feels magnetic and deeply familiar, yet it can bring emotional highs and lows that are challenging to navigate. You might feel an instant sense of recognition when you meet, as if you have known each other forever. There is often an overwhelming need to be together, even when circumstances make it difficult.

****

I want to share a few final thoughts on this topic.

Love is a beautiful force, but let's be honest — love alone is not enough to sustain a lasting and fulfilling relationship! If it were, the global divorce rate would be much lower. Despite our best efforts to find that one perfect counterpart, we are failing on a grand scale, with over a dozen countries now officially surpassing the 50 percent mark in divorce rates. That is a staggering number.

Divorces can get ugly. The emotional toll is often immense, not just for the couple but especially for any children involved. Children feel it more deeply because they rely on both parents for their emotional and physical stability. That kind of disruption cuts deep.

Now, here is a practical suggestion that could help you reduce the risk of getting a divorce or avoid it altogether. If you are in a serious relationship, consider living together for at least two years before getting married. Be intentional about not getting pregnant during that time, so that neither party feels pressured into marriage.

Take the time to observe how your relationship functions on a daily basis; your shared routines and responsibilities, how you handle conflict, how well you communicate, and whether your values remain in harmony.

If, after this period, you still feel deeply connected, fulfilled, and in sync with one another, then marriage may naturally emerge as the next logical step.

From my own observations, couples who moved in together and married within a year and a half had a noticeably higher divorce rate than those who waited at least two years. Time has a way of revealing things that the honeymoon phase tends to hide.

I am not a relationship expert and do not offer definitive answers on matters of the heart. But I do hope that this bit of insight offers something of value. Sometimes, a little practical wisdom can go a long way.

"The mind, once stretched by a new idea, never returns to its original dimensions."

— Ralph Waldo Emerson

CHAPTER 22

Epilogue: Embody What You Know and Trust the Process

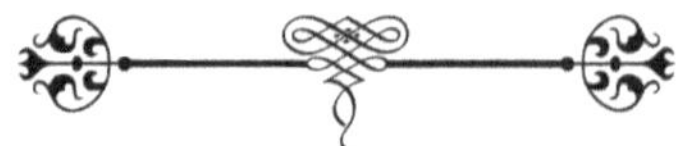

Writing this book was a journey in itself. It was my first official publication, and I poured every ounce of myself into it. I wanted it to be accurate, honest, and helpful. More than that, I wanted it to be genuine. I wanted to ensure that you had everything I wished someone had given me at the start of my journey.

My aim was to share tools and knowledge that have genuinely transformed my life. I wanted to be thorough, clear, and practical, ensuring that the concepts, some ancient and some newly framed, could be immediately helpful. I imagine your journey through these pages has been one of discovery, perhaps challenging, but hopefully deeply rewarding.

As we reach the final chapter of this book, I would like to take a moment to reflect with you and acknowledge how far we have come together.

You have been introduced to the idea that there are many Higher Sources of Knowledge and Wisdom that can be accessed and support us. You have learned how to connect with them, how to use self-muscle testing as a divination tool, and how to develop a real and empowering relationship with your Higher Self.

A substantial part of our time was dedicated to mastering self-muscle testing. My goal was to guide you step by step, providing detailed explanations and illustrations on how to become truly proficient, troubleshoot possible issues, and explore countless general and advanced applications.

By accessing a Higher Source of Knowledge and Wisdom and using self-muscle testing, you can find the clearest, most aligned path forward, whether it involves relationships, career, health, or spiritual growth.

The skills you have cultivated are potent. You now have a direct method to explore what helps you reach your full potential, to identify what is truly in your highest good in any given moment, and to understand what your body and spirit genuinely need and when.

You now hold a skill set that can serve you for the rest of your life if practiced with integrity, balance, and trust.

I wish to expand on my last statement, not as an author, but as a fellow traveler on the path of growth, truth, and self-discovery. In your pursuit of answers, do not fall into the trap of needing to control everything. I have made this mistake. I once reached a point where I was testing every single decision, every opportunity, every little fork in the road. I became obsessed with certainty, but that came with consequences. It drained me and dulled my intuition rather than sharpening it!

Then one day, a serious businessperson came into my practice as a patient and impressed me with his sharp appearance, luxurious car, and extensive knowledge of investing. Eventually, I inquired about the type of investment packages he was offering and how the high yield on the investment was justified. At that stage, I was tired of testing and realized that I had become dependent on it. So I said to myself, "Fuck it. I am not testing this one." I proceeded to make a decision based on logic and excitement, just as I had in the past. That decision turned out to be a painful one, not just for me, but for close friends I had brought in. We all lost a significant part of our savings, and I lost something more valuable: some of my best friends who had put their trust in me. It was a hard and humbling lesson. 😟

So here is my advice to you, from someone who has lived on both sides of the spectrum: do not become a slave to needing to know everything in advance. That need to control every outcome will only drain you and stunt your growth. Balance is the key. You were never meant to control everything. Life still requires trust, surrender, and the courage to leap. Self-muscle testing is a divination tool. Use it wisely. Let it guide you toward your highest good, not into obsession.

In every misstep I have made, I have taken the time to reflect on and meditate upon it, identifying all the lessons that came with it. Every mistake made me stronger and wiser.

And now for some uplifting news. The more you practice self-muscle testing using the extensive approach, the more you can expect your primary clairs to awaken. We are speaking, of course, about your clairvoyance, clairaudience, clairsentience, and claircognizance.

You may begin to notice that, at the moment of receiving a yes or no answer, additional information becomes available. You might perceive an image, or perhaps an inner explanation justifying the answer. This is a fantastic experience that can lead to eliminating the need for self-muscle testing altogether!

God, I love my exclamation marks and happy faces! 😊! 😊 ! 😊 !

Thank you for investing your precious time and energy in these pages, for trusting me to be your guide, for applying what you have learned, and for choosing to grow. Keep learning, and never stop becoming the person you were always meant to be.

Above all, I truly commend you. Your deep commitment to personal growth and reaching your full potential is admirable. The journey of self-development is ongoing, and you have equipped yourself with powerful tools to navigate it with greater clarity and confidence. May you use them wisely, find your balance, and build a life that reflects the very best of who you are.

Finally, if I may, I would like to ask for a small favor. If you have found value in these pages, I would be incredibly grateful if you could take a moment to leave a brief and honest review. Just a few words about your experience, what you found helpful or not, what resonated and what did not, or anything you think might guide other readers. Your voice might just be the one that inspires someone else to begin their journey. Thank you for considering this.

With deep appreciation, gratitude, and love,
GCG

APPENDIX A

Deep Conscious Harmonious Breathing

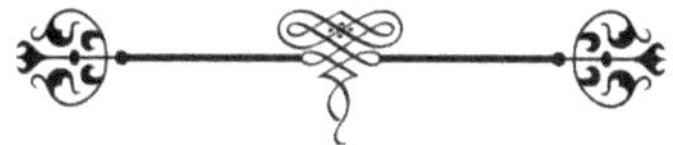

**An explanation of this breathing technique can be found in Chapter 10.4.

Instructions:

Make sure you are in a calm environment. Turn off any music or background noise and silence your phone. You may choose to sit or lie down, with your eyes open or closed. Go with what feels most comfortable for you.

Simply start by breathing a little deeper than usual and more consciously, meaning you notice how the air enters and leaves your body and how each inhale and exhale affects different parts of you.

As your breathing awareness deepens, you begin to realize that your breathing is something you can control. You can choose to breathe through your mouth, your nose, or both. You can take in a full breath or a shallow one. You begin to see that you have options.

Among all these options, you naturally choose what feels most harmonious to you. The traits of harmonious breathing are simple. It brings a natural smile to your face and causes no strain while you breathe. At the same time, you remain consciously aware of each breath, allowing it to be slightly deeper than usual.

And that's really the essence of this practice: to arrive at a place where you smile and just be. Once you have reached this state, stay with it for as long as you like. It is in this space that you can hear us clearly and begin to engage in a genuine conversation.

APPENDIX B
Grounding and Neutralization Technique

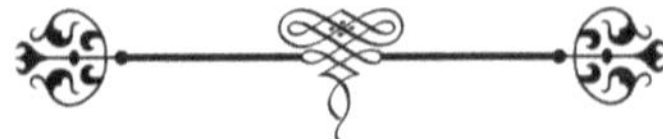

Instructions:

Find a comfortable seated position. Gently close your eyes and bring your attention to the lower part of your pelvis, at your Root Chakra. (For guidance on the Root Chakra location, see Appendix D)

Begin with Deep, Conscious, Harmonious Breathing, keeping your eyes closed.

Visualize and feel multiple red-colored roots emerging from your Root Chakra, growing downward and entering deep into Mother Earth. See or sense these roots traveling at least 30 feet or 10 meters beneath the surface, anchoring you firmly into the Earth. If you are seated above ground level in a building, imagine your roots growing longer, effortlessly reaching all the way to the Earth below.

Now, imagine yourself as a magnificent ancient tree, with a huge trunk, sprawling branches, and vibrant green leaves. Feel yourself unaffected by even the harshest winds and changing seasons, emotionally impervious to external changes, standing tall and resilient through time.

Now, shift your focus to the deep bond between you and Mother Earth. Allow yourself to feel Mother Earth's unconditional love, nourishment, and strength rising up through your roots and filling you.

In this moment, simply be. No judgments, no emotions, no expectations.

Stay in this state for a few minutes.

When you are ready, gently bring your awareness back to the present moment, carrying with you the grounded peace and strength you have received.

APPENDIX C

The 8th Gateway Technique

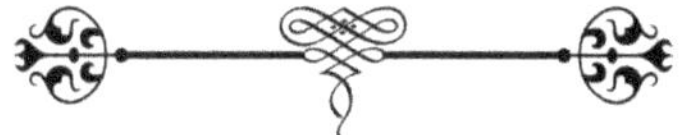

Begin by sitting upright, either in a chair or on the floor in your preferred meditation posture, ensuring your spine is straight and relaxed.

Begin with Deep, Conscious, Harmonious Breathing, keeping your eyes closed.

Once you are centered, visualize your Higher Self Chakra located 6 to 7 inches (15 to 18 centimeters) above the crown of the head, glowing as a radiant, white, etheric sphere, about 3 inches in diameter.

Hold your attention there as you continue your Deep Conscious Harmonious Breathing.

Next, visualize, or better yet, sense yourself sitting at the center of a large four-sided energetic pyramid. This pyramid has no walls, only a glowing white radiating energy frame.

Now visualize a thick beam of brilliant light descending from above. It enters through the pyramid's apex through an opening, flows through your Higher Self Chakra, and continues downward all the way to the base of your Sushumna Nadi. The beam remains steady and unmoving throughout the meditation. The source of this light is your Over Soul, but if it feels more natural to see it coming from the Source of All That Is, the Universe, or any other divine origin, it is fine.

Take a few moments to feel the energy and structures you have activated.

Then affirm:
- I am one with my Higher Self.
- I am whole.
- I am one with all that is.

Then chant the mantra **OM SHANTI OM** at least 13 times, feeling its vibration expand and strengthen the Higher Self Chakra and your entire energetic system.

When you finish, you have several options.

You may choose to rest in this state of deep meditative absorption, also known as **Samadhi** in yogic tradition. You can also use this heightened state to ask questions and receive answers intuitively, or use muscle testing to receive instant guidance from your selected Higher Source.

At times, you may notice or sense the pyramid structure beginning to rotate, either clockwise or counterclockwise. This movement is completely natural, and you should allow it to unfold without resistance. It simply reflects energetic shifts occurring within you, such as alignment, activation, or transformation.

APPENDIX D

The 8 main chakras and the *Sushumna Nadi*

"Our goal is to recognize, awaken, and cultivate our full potential, so we may evolve into the enlightened human beings we are all destined to become."

— George C. Georgiou

www.ingramcontent.com/pod-product-compliance
Lightning Source LLC
LaVergne TN
LVHW081300100826
845148LV00005B/929
9789925823833